"If you're struggling with self-esteem, then loo [illegible] this groundbreaking book, which will help you to appreciate yourself from a whole new perspective. In this clear and practical guide based on the latest behavioral science, Joe Oliver and Richard Bennett have skilfully laid out all the steps needed for you to build a more nurturing relationship with yourself, and a life of greater meaning and purpose. I highly recommend this book."

—**Mike Sinclair, DPsych**, clinical director of City Psychology Group, and coauthor of *Mindfulness for Busy People*, *The Little ACT Workbook*, and *The Little Depression Workbook*

"Ready for a new perspective on self-esteem? Joe and Rich provide a perfect balance of confrontation, compassion, practical worksheets, audio exercises, and engaging examples to wake us up to the fact that human beings are amazing—and that includes YOU. This succinct, well-documented book is perhaps the best book in the mindfulness and acceptance workbook series; a definite must-read for humans seeking freedom and authenticity."

—**Patti Robinson, PhD**, international consultant and trainer, and coauthor of *The Mindfulness and Acceptance Workbook for Depression*

"If you are struggling in the grip of your self-story, but still can't work out who you really are, this book is for you. It's thorough, based on solid concepts and methods, and yet totally readable. It is packed with clear, helpful diagrams and exercises to guide you toward adopting a workable, transformative, self-compassionate stance with regard to who you are and what you experience."

—**Yvonne Barnes-Holmes, PhD**, associate professor in behavior analysis, and senior researcher at Ghent University; and author of over 150 articles on behavioral science

"The authors of this fabulous workbook have a story to tell, and if you listen to it and learn from it, it will change your life. In a remarkably practical, humble, and genuine way, the authors tell us a story about living with the joys and sorrows of wanting to belong, of wanting to fit in, of wanting to care about and be cared for by others. This workbook teaches you how to stand tall in the presence of these vital human pursuits, to accept your anxieties and self-doubts, and to act according to your personal values. Above all, this workbook will teach you that it is pointless to search for self-esteem and self-acceptance, because you already have it. It was given to you as a birthright. This book will teach you how to reclaim it! Highly recommended!"

—**Kirk Strosahl, PhD**, codeveloper of acceptance and commitment therapy (ACT), and coauthor of *The Mindfulness and Acceptance Workbook for Depression*

"*The Mindfulness and Acceptance Workbook for Self-Esteem* by Oliver and Bennett is a beautifully crafted, interactive book with touching personal stories of the authors' own self-esteem, leading on through innovative exercises that use cutting-edge theory from psychological sciences. They help the reader to understand self-esteem and how we can run into trouble with our self-esteem in an accessible way. The workbook is ideal to help anyone strengthen their most important relationship, that is, the relationship with our self."

—**Louise McHugh, PhD**, professor in the school of psychology at University College Dublin; peer-reviewed ACT trainer; author of over one hundred academic papers in the area of ACT and relational frame theory (RFT); and coauthor of *The Self and Perspective Taking* and *A Contextual Behavioral Guide to the Self*

"There is a world of wisdom packed into this accessible, elegant workbook. The authors pursue psychology's Holy Grail—self-esteem—and deliver it to the reader, step by step. Or rather, they draw upon empirical research, their considerable clinical experience, and even their own lives to show why efforts to obtain and hold on to a thing called 'self-esteem' don't work—offering instead a way to build a sense of self that is accepting, compassionate, and ultimately freeing. This is the sort of text that should be required reading for us all."

—**Darrah Westrup, PhD**, author of *Advanced Acceptance and Commitment Therapy*; and coauthor of *Acceptance and Commitment Therapy for the Treatment of Post-Traumatic Stress Disorder and Trauma-Related Problems*, *The Mindful Couple*, and *Learning ACT for Group Treatment*

"Joe Oliver and Richard Bennett are well known for publications and training that have both a solid foundation in contextual behavioral science (CBS), and are easy for readers to absorb. This book will give readers the opportunity to loosen from some of their old self-talk, and create bigger lives."

—**Louise Hayes, PhD**, clinical psychologist; and coauthor of *The Thriving Adolescent*; *Your Life, Your Way*; and *Get Out of Your Mind and Into Your Life for Teens*

"The solution to low self-esteem sits hidden in a place you'd never think to look. This book shows you where that place is, and how to use your greater freedom from self-criticism to take your life in a new direction. Gentle, witty, and wise—the book feels like a conversation with a helpful friend. If self-esteem is a struggle for you, do yourself a favor and read this book."

—**Steven C. Hayes, PhD**, Nevada Foundation Professor in the department of psychology at the University of Nevada, Reno; and originator and codeveloper of ACT

The Mindfulness & Acceptance Workbook for Self-Esteem

Using Acceptance & Commitment Therapy to Move Beyond Negative Self-Talk & Embrace Self-Compassion

JOE OLIVER, PHD
RICHARD BENNETT, CLINPSYD

New Harbinger Publications, Inc.

Publisher's Note

This publication is designed to provide accurate and authoritative information in regard to the subject matter covered. It is sold with the understanding that the publisher is not engaged in rendering psychological, financial, legal, or other professional services. If expert assistance or counseling is needed, the services of a competent professional should be sought.

NEW HARBINGER PUBLICATIONS is a registered trademark of New Harbinger Publications, Inc.

Distributed in Canada by Raincoast Books

Copyright © 2020 by Joe Oliver and Richard Bennett
New Harbinger Publications, Inc.
5674 Shattuck Avenue
Oakland, CA 94609
www.newharbinger.com

"A Song for Damian Marquez the Tailor," by Ancient Champion, used for the "Mindfulness of Sound" activity in chapter 7, is copyright Ancient Champion (Paul Lamont). Used with permission.

Cover design by Amy Shoup; Acquired by Tesilya Hanauer;
Edited by Rona Bernstein; Illustrations by Louise Gardner

All Rights Reserved

Library of Congress Cataloging-in-Publication Data

Names: Oliver, Joseph E., author. | Bennett, Richard (Psychologist), author.
Title: The mindfulness and acceptance workbook for self-esteem / Joe Oliver and Richard Bennett.
Description: Oakland, CA : New Harbinger Publications, [2020] | Includes bibliographical references.
Identifiers: LCCN 2020011247 (print) | LCCN 2020011248 (ebook) | ISBN 9781684033041 (trade paperback) | ISBN 9781684033058 (pdf) | ISBN 9781684033065 (epub)
Subjects: LCSH: Self-esteem. | Acceptance and commitment therapy. | Mindfulness (Psychology)
Classification: LCC BF697.5.S46 O47 2020 (print) | LCC BF697.5.S46 (ebook) | DDC 158.1--dc23
LC record available at https://lccn.loc.gov/2020011247
LC ebook record available at https://lccn.loc.gov/2020011248

Printed in the United States of America

24 23 22

10 9 8 7 6 5 4 3 2

Contents

Foreword

When Joe Oliver and Richard Bennett invited me to write this foreword, my immediate reaction was joy, gratitude, and an instant "Yes, I'd be delighted." Unfortunately, this reaction didn't last. When I actually sat down to write this foreword, my mind kicked in with a whole load of unhelpful self-talk: "You don't know how to write a foreword. Everything you write will be boring and you'll just look stupid." And so on, and so on. If I'd let those thoughts dictate my actions…well, for sure this foreword would never have been written. The good news is, within the pages of this book, Joe and Rich describe numerous tools and techniques for rapidly taking the power out of harsh, judgmental self-talk. So, I quickly applied a couple of them, that critical inner voice instantly lost its impact, and I was able to get on with writing.

The inconvenient truth is, in the Western world, we have become increasingly obsessed with the need for high self-esteem. Teachers and parents tell children, "You need it"; friends confide in each other, "I don't have it"; and clients ask their therapists, "How can I get it?" But what actually is self-esteem? And is it really all it's cracked up to be? Is it truly that important? Do we really "need it" to have a good life? Is all this emphasis on building self-esteem actually healthy? And do the methods commonly proposed really work?

Well, as you've probably guessed, you'll soon find out the answers to these questions. And I urge you, as you read these pages, to please keep an open mind, because you're going to discover that a lot of what you think you know about self-esteem just ain't so.

For example, you're going to discover that low self-esteem has an upside, and high self-esteem has a downside—and that the simplistic idea that the former is bad and the latter is good doesn't hold up to scientific scrutiny. That's just for starters. From those unsettling beginnings, the authors are going to take you step-by-step through a new scientific approach to dealing with the whole issue of self-esteem, an approach that's radically different from all those pop psychology ideas you've encountered so often. For example, you will *not* find anything about how to think positively, focus on all your good points, challenge your negative thoughts, or rehearse positive affirmations.

What you will find instead is how to develop a deep sense of self-acceptance and self-compassion, using a scientific, evidence-based model of psychotherapy known as acceptance and commitment therapy (ACT). The ACT approach will help you develop an authentic, kind, and caring connection with yourself and a deep sense of self-worth that's a world apart from anything you might hope to achieve through positive thinking and rehearsing affirmations.

So, here's hoping I've whetted your appetite for the life-changing journey ahead of you. It's very painful in some parts, very funny in others, and overall, inspiring and transformative. Good luck with it all and have some fun along the way. I'm leaving you in good hands.

Cheers,
Russ Harris
Author of *ACT Made Simple* and *The Happiness Trap*

Introduction

Here's a fact—we humans love a good story. We can't help but get sucked in, especially to ones with drama, heartache, and adventure. Which ones really catch our attention? It's real stories about *people* that are the most engaging. So, we thought a good place to start would be stories about us...

JOE'S STORY

I grew up feeling on the outside of everything. I often had the sense that I was standing in the cold, watching everyone inside gathered around, talking, laughing, and enjoying each other's company. I desperately wanted to be on the inside, but somehow, no matter what I did, I couldn't work out how to get there. I figured it was something that was wrong with me. I wasn't smart enough, funny enough, interesting enough—I just wasn't *enough*. It's a feeling that I remember from since I was about six years old. For the longest time, I didn't even realize I was carrying this story with me. I just *knew* I wasn't enough. I didn't even stop to question it. As life went by, I worked really hard to try and hide that I wasn't enough. I pushed myself and set super high standards for myself, which meant I achieved some good things. However, I ground myself down and was very hard on myself. At other points, I just gave up and withdrew from everyone, which was easy to do. As an only child, I was comfy in my own company, but it was easy to become lonely and disconnected.

Slowly, through a lot of therapy, reading self-help books, and talking with loving friends, family, and my wife, I came to realize that this *story* about my not being enough was there. I gradually came to understand how I interacted with it, listened to it, and gave in to it, and how doing so kept me safe. I eventually came to see just how limiting it was to my life. From this point, I was able to make real changes in my life. Slowing down, not being so hard on myself, and allowing myself to be vulnerable enough to open up to others were some of the real game changers. The story stopped owning me and I started to own the story.

RICHARD'S STORY

I'm going to tell this story in reverse. This is because I'm sitting in front of my laptop having just read Joe's story for the first time. My mind is kicking off. It's saying that I have to come up with something as open, honest, vulnerable, and inspiring as the passage that Joe has just sent me. The thing is, I think he is just better at this stuff than me. Well, not just this stuff...everything. And he's not alone up on that pedestal. My mind tells me that pretty much everyone I care about is better at most things than I am. Somehow, somewhere along the line in my history, I developed a story about myself. It's about not being wise or capable enough to make a success of anything important. This story is very old and has held me back in a number of different ways.

There are certain things in my history that I can point to as being important in shaping my version of the "not good enough" story. I give myself a hard time about that too. My mind says that there is no good reason for thinking these thoughts and, therefore, I have no right to feel bad. This story doesn't show up in every situation, and yet it feels very familiar. So familiar that I've often just accepted it as the truth. Taking it literally has led me to feel like I need to protect myself against it, and I've developed a well-worn tendency to avoid situations where "not good enough" thoughts might show up. I would like to say it's gotten better as I've grown older and wiser, but that wouldn't be entirely true. It's still a work in progress. I'm slowly learning that letting this story run the show not only doesn't help, it makes things worse. Accepting it and learning to live alongside it is the thing that has helped me the most.

HOW TO APPROACH THIS BOOK

The stories we tell ourselves about who we are will form a big part of this book. These stories are not made up of myths or fables, but rather are living, breathing narratives that we interact with every day. We want to help you see your story and understand its history and how you relate to it. Together, we want to help you choose your *own* relationship with your story and yourself.

Although we both work as clinical psychologists, it certainly doesn't mean we are on the top of the mountain, dispensing words of wisdom on how you can catch up to where we are. Rather, as you can probably sense from our stories above, we are both still climbing our own mountains, just as you climb yours. Perhaps what we have is a different perspective. From over on our mountains, we can see your mountain differently and with a little distance. We can offer you what we hope is a fresh and useful perspective on your climb. Perhaps some useful tips, suggestions, and ways for you to continue your journey onward and upward, while enjoying the view. And, let's not forget, if we were to encounter each other in different circumstances, you could probably do the same thing for us.

We've divided this book into three sections. Part 1 begins by focusing on our self-esteem stories and how to make sense of them. We'll introduce you to the concept of self-acceptance and set the scene for moving from wanting "high" self-esteem to a place of accepting who you already are. In Part 2, we'll describe a self-care starting point, which will help you get ready for making changes, think about how to build a good foundation, and learn ways to be kind and compassionate in this process. Finally, in Part 3, we will take you through our six steps to self-acceptance, which will help you build the kind of life *you* want, rather than the life your mind and your thoughts tell you that you can have.

At the end of each chapter, you will find a "Bringing It All Together" box, where we will invite you to pause for a moment before moving forward. This is to help you introduce some breathing space to take on board what you've read and learned. We hope that completing these short exercises will help you gain more perspective and focus on the changes you want to make in your own life.

We've packed the book with the kinds of exercises, worksheets, and metaphors that we use regularly when offering therapy to people. They are the tools that have helped people to make real changes in their lives. Many of the exercises and worksheets, as well as several audio files, are available to download from the website for this book at http://www.newharbinger.com/43041. (See the very back of this book for more details.) Our invitation to you is to dive in and give them a go. The easy thing to do would be to skim through the exercises and think, *I'll come back and do them later.* But just like learning any new skill, it's putting in the practice that really matters. It's one of life's tough facts, and it's only by stepping out of your comfort zone that you get the opportunity to build the kind of life you really want.

PART 1

Making Sense of Self-Esteem

CHAPTER 1

A Brief History of the Human Race: The Need to Fit In with the Group

We are going to begin this book in the last place that you would probably expect us to. Your mind might protest when you see where we are going to start, and we urge you to make a courageous move and stick with it. Ready? Strap yourself in. Here goes...

You are amazing.

You're still here? That's a relief. Well done. We imagine those three words might be grating on you right now. That's probably because there's a good chance that you don't always feel amazing, and feeling *pretty far from amazing* may even be the reason that you reached for this book in the first place. Nevertheless, it is our contention that there is something really amazing about you. And we would really like you to stick around a while longer as we explain just how amazing you are and how it is that you got to be that way. It all started a very long time ago...

THE EVOLUTION OF HUMAN SOCIETY

Scientists believe that humans have been around for about 250,000 years. Although there are various explanations about how we all got here, there is no dispute that human beings differ significantly from most of the other creatures we share the planet with. This is where we come back to the idea of you being amazing. Along with the rest of your fellow humans, you are capable of things that no other creature on Earth will ever be able to achieve. You have a talent for the most incredibly creative and flexible patterns of thought and behavior. You can create entire worlds in your imagination and effortlessly travel from the past to the future. Up there in that head, you can conjure incredible beauty and the most fearsome monsters. Your brain is the biological equivalent of a high-performance sports car. It leaves the rest of the field standing. Just like with that sports car, it would probably be wise to understand a little of how your brain works before you take it out for a spin.

This leads us to an interesting story featuring, among other things, fire, food, and friends. By the way, if your mind is grating on you again at this point, perhaps saying stuff like *Well, I can buy that human beings as a species are pretty remarkable, but me, I'm just useless,* later chapters are going to unpack further why you, our dear reader holding this book right now, are personally amazing yourself. Stick with us.

For most of our history, humans lived in small groups, slowly developing more and more complex ways of living. We were largely nomadic until about 12,000 years ago, when we started planting and growing crops. Once agriculture was born, we needed to stay in one place in order to look after our harvest. In turn, this necessitated the building of walls to keep other communities out and a whole host of new technologies to build, maintain, and run these new settlements. Gradually, we started to develop specialized skill sets. Where previously, individuals in hunter-gatherer bands would have *all* been strong, athletic, and equipped with the skills for survival on the move, people living in settlements began to specialize. As our villages, towns, and eventually cities became ever more complex, a wide range of occupational roles came into being and we developed myriad new ways to interact with, and relate to, each other.

In the modern age, our division of labor and roles has made us stronger as a group, although as individuals we have moved from knowing pretty much everything we needed to know for our survival to becoming highly skilled in just one or two areas. For example, you might be fantastic at performing open-heart surgery while having no clue whatsoever about how to grow tomatoes. Since there are countless people in our society who are better than us at lots of different tasks (neither of us are very good at open-heart surgery *or* growing tomatoes), for the individual person, this leaves lots of room for feelings of inadequacy to creep in and take hold. In terms of the whole of human history, this transition, along with other changes to the way we live, has been extremely rapid, and modern humans, with the same brains as their Stone Age ancestors, often find themselves struggling to keep up with the pace of it all.

COOPERATION

You might be wondering what on Earth this history lesson has to do with the way you feel about yourself. The key to the answer is buried in the previous paragraph and relates to the unique ability of humans to cooperate in the way that we do. Let's pause for a moment to consider who has cooperated to put this humble little book in your hands. We'll start with you. Clearly you are central to the notion of "you reading this book." Before you, there are us, the authors. Between you and us, there are the wonderful editors Tesilya and Vicraj. They work for the publisher, New Harbinger, and have been our main point of contact during the writing process. There are yet others involved in proofreading, printing, and distribution before you can get your hands on a physical copy of the book. You might be reading a digital copy, which means a whole bunch of other people in the chain. The thing is, it doesn't really stop there. We wrote the book on computers, and neither of us built those machines ourselves. Thousands of people have cooperated to invent, design, build, and distribute our laptops. In formulating our ideas, we talked on the phone, chatted online, and met up in person. That's thousands more people right there from the communication, marketing, retail, and transport industries. And then there are all the people like teachers, colleagues, and clients who influenced our careers, and all the people who have shaped *your* life, for good or ill, to the point where you thought you might be interested in picking up this book. Now, obviously, the vast majority of those people were not doing what they did with the specific intention of facilitating your reading this book; however, if we take any of them out of the equation, "you reading this book" may never have happened. Such is the incredible nature of human cooperation. We do things together that benefit people we have never even met or who perhaps are not even born yet. It really is an amazing thing. Imagine how many people's destinies you have touched in the course of your life, either directly or indirectly, through your personal life or your work. If we gathered them all together in one room, how big would that room have to be?

LANGUAGE AND COMMUNICATION

This ability to cooperate has helped human beings compensate for our numerous physical disadvantages. We cannot fly, breathe under water, or survive for long in extreme temperatures. Our senses are not that acute, and our bodies are relatively small and frail. However, we *are* able to flexibly cooperate on a huge scale—and that has set us apart and contributed to our success. So, how did we achieve that? One theory suggests that about 70,000 years ago, human brain development took a leap forward and we developed the kind of abstract thinking and language abilities that we take for granted today. This enabled us to communicate with much greater precision and was the spark that ignited an explosion in the development of better tools and more complex cultural practices. In his book about human history, *Sapiens,* Yuval Noah Harari (2014) lists three key benefits of this major development in communication. Having advanced language capabilities means that (1) we are able to learn quickly, (2) we can pass on that knowledge to others across generations, and (3) those whom we pass that knowledge to are able to build and expand on it, developing greater insights along the way.

Let's look at one example that we've all been through. Many years back, someone taught you to cross the road. Crossing the road is risky business, and someone who had previously learned the trick to doing it safely passed that knowledge on to you. They probably did this using language, alongside some actual demonstration of how to get across safely. We are willing to bet that they didn't pick you up and throw you in front of an oncoming vehicle in order for you to experience firsthand the consequences of not crossing safely. This is the great benefit of language in terms of cooperation. You can learn things without having to be shown. You can learn that roads are dangerous without having to actually get run over. The thing is, we need others to show us these skills. Therefore, being part of a social group is, and always has been, incredibly important to our survival. Historically, this has been a matter of life and death: if we were cast out of the group, we would usually wind up dead before too long. One might argue that our social nature is even more important today because of the specialization that has developed in modern society. We are all much more dependent on each other's skills for survival, whether that be in relation to tomato farming, heart surgery, or anything else.

THE DARK SIDE OF LANGUAGE

We all play a part in the incredible achievements of humanity. On a daily basis, we bend the environment to our will and contribute to complex systems of culture, religion, and commerce. Even our infant children can do things that no other creature on the planet will do in its lifetime. The power, flexibility, and creativity that language has given us is an incredible gift. However, language can also work against us and hold us back in ways that other species never have to worry about.

Let's go back to your learning to cross the road without ever having to get run over by a vehicle. What basically happened there was that you learned to be anxious about something that had never actually happened. In terms of not being run over, this is a good thing—your anxiety helped you to be cautious and pay attention each time you cross the road. The trouble is that being anxious about things that have never actually happened can show up in all sorts of ways that are definitely not so good. Have you ever worried about an upcoming event? Lost sleep over something that was due to happen the following week? Avoided something because your mind had convinced you that it would turn out badly? These kinds of experiences can be less helpful. They are uniquely human. Antelope don't worry about whether there will be enough food to eat *tomorrow.* Sheep tend not to ruminate over their past mistakes. Tigers don't give a moment's thought to how their careers are going to pan out. And zebras don't get stress-related illnesses, as Robert Sapolsky's (2004) famous book, *Why Zebras Don't Get Ulcers,* illustrates.

As much as human language is a gift, it does have a darker side. It can exert a huge amount of control over our behavior, and as we get older, we increasingly see the world not directly *as it is,* but as our minds *tell us it is.* We perceive the world through the filter of our thoughts, most of which are built out of words. Consequently, we struggle to be mindful and present-focused in the way that other animals seem to do so effortlessly. Animals without complex language abilities tend to respond to what is directly happening in their environment. If a cow in a farmer's field brushes against an electrified fence, it will move away from that fence as quickly as it can, and you would be unlikely to find many cows leaning against electrified fences. As humans, we *can* respond like this, although our minds tend to give us other things to respond to that are not about our direct experience. For example, you might stay in an unhappy relationship because of thoughts like *No one else would ever want me*, even though *experience* tells you that other people have indeed found you attractive as a person. We allow our minds to dictate to us what matters, and we respond to imagined consequences instead of actual ones. This can turn into the equivalent of leaning against the electrified fence.

Within human history, we can see how the development of spoken language facilitated the spread of ideas and stories, and that this gathered pace even more quickly with the advent of the written word. Over time, for both individuals and groups, ideas and stories can grow in stature, and if there is a clash between the stories and actual experience, the story often wins. There are numerous examples of this all around us. Have you ever encountered a bureaucratic or administrative system that hasn't received your forms or has recorded the wrong information about you? Generally, it is the information "in the system" that will be trusted over anything that you might say or do. You may have been judged or selected or rejected for something on the basis of your academic grades at some point. Using information in this way to tell stories about people didn't exist until a few hundred years ago, and yet it can determine the way that other people perceive you—or, if you are like most people, that you perceive yourself. You might have decided that you are not good enough based on some arbitrary criteria like your grade point average or your bank balance. Language, and the ideas and stories that it can create, shapes an enormous amount of our daily experience.

As language has taken over in human society, one of the consequences for us as inherently social creatures has been that we use it to compare ourselves to other people, and most often, we judge ourselves as coming up short in one way or another. The rapid pace of societal change has contributed to the inexorable rise of this rating game. If we consider our Stone Age roots, the evidence suggests that humans lived in small groups of approximately thirty to fifty hunter-gatherers. If you were a member of this community, your social reference group was small by modern standards. There were fewer people to compare yourself to. If you were a woman in her early twenties looking for a mate, your reference group was even smaller. If the entire community numbered only fifty, there would have been very few women in their early twenties besides you, perhaps only four or five. Back then it would have been much harder to look around the group and decide that you were inferior. Fast forward to today, and a woman in her twenties probably sees way more than four or five other twenty-something women before she even arrives at her place of study or work. If you add in all the comparable women she will see on social media, television, billboards, and magazines during the day, the number could easily be in the hundreds. If we also consider that many of those images will be retouched and airbrushed to conform with somebody's view of perfection, we can start to see how much easier it is to look around at others and decide we are not good enough.

A concrete example of this phenomenon occurred in Fiji in the 1990s, when television arrived for the first time. In Fijian society, having a fuller or more robust figure was traditionally deemed an attractive feature in both men and women, whereas being of slim build was associated with being weak. However, within three years of the arrival of television, which brought with it the portrayal of Western images and values, many women started to think of themselves as being too big, and diagnosable eating disorders appeared for the first time.

The human population has rapidly expanded from approximately half a billion in the year 1500 to around seven billion today. Our brains have changed little since the Stone Age, and it is no wonder that we struggle to keep up with the complexity of the world around us. If you have ever looked around at other people and decided that you are not good enough or that you don't fit in with the group, history suggests there are some good reasons why you might have done that, and you are most definitely not alone.

THE HUMAN CONDITION: WE HURT WHERE WE CARE

One of the consequences of wanting something a lot is worrying about not having it. Caring about anything tends to be closely related to getting stressed about it. Take a moment to think about the person you love most in the entire world (you can pick more than one if you feel like you're having to choose!). There's a good chance that this same person also has the power to make you more anxious or angry than anybody else. Care and hurt, value and pain, all wrapped up in the same relationship. In exactly the same way, wanting to be part of the group will be closely related to worrying that you are not really part of it. This is why most of us have a version of the "I'm not good enough" story running around in our heads. As human beings, we desperately want to belong, and the flip side of that is a deep-rooted anxiety that we don't. It is important to remember that we are most likely descended from the more anxious of the Stone Age people, since those who were more cautious and more on the lookout for various sources of threat were more likely to survive and reproduce. While they are often uncomfortable, anxiety and doubt are very natural parts of the human experience. To paraphrase the writer and comedian Ruby Wax, your brain is designed to keep you alive; it "couldn't give a shit about your happiness" ("Ruby Wax Talks" 2015).

THE QUEST FOR SELF-ESTEEM

A thought like *I'm not good enough* is a prime example of the language of low self-esteem. It's hard to imagine having that thought and then punching the air with joy. It's likely to make you feel bad and have a negative impact on your confidence and motivation. Since the publication of Nathaniel Branden's (1969) *The Psychology of Self-Esteem*, mainstream psychology and the mass media have been fascinated by the concept of self-esteem, and it is often used to describe how people see themselves. It is not uncommon for therapists to refer to their clients as "having" low self-esteem, almost as if it were a disease.

If we pick it apart, the term "self-esteem" has two components. First, there is the "self" part. We could disappear down a very large and complex rabbit hole trying to define exactly what the self is, although for simplicity we might think of it as everything that goes into making you *you*. It is the summation of all your behaviors, emotions, thoughts, sensations, and urges. In combination, these things make up a story of who you are. The story is mostly stable across time and is often the object of our introspection and navel-gazing, which is where the "esteem" part comes in. The word "esteem" comes from the verb "estimate" and signifies a judgment or evaluation. These days, "esteem" is most often used as a noun, interchangeable with words like "worth." It follows that coming to a view about your self-esteem involves an evaluation of your *entire* self. Now, it might not be what you are expecting to hear, but we have a problem with that...

We believe that you are too amazing to be evaluated in such a simple and all-encompassing way. How could we reasonably come up with a judgment of you that captures all of your complexity? A big part of the notion of low self-esteem is that it involves globally rating ourselves with judgments like *I'm not good enough*. It's like saying "I" = "not good enough." This doesn't really cut it. Not good enough at what? Not good enough for whom? Not good enough when, or in what situation? The wonderfully complicated and ever-evolving person that you are is just too complex to be given a single rating like that. "Not good enough" is just not up to the task of describing you, or anyone else on the planet.

If you want to play with this idea a little, consider the chair that you are sitting in. If you are not sitting in a chair, go and find one. Be kind to yourself and take the load off for a few minutes. Then, take a moment to look that chair up and down. Get acquainted with how it feels to sit in it. Do you think you could come up with a single word or phrase that can successfully evaluate the whole chair? Something that completely captures the essence of the chair? Have a go. We've even started the sentence for you.

This chair is ____.

Now, we are prepared to bet that if you came up with something, it probably does a good job of describing a *quality* of the chair or some *particular aspect* of it. You might have said, "This chair is comfortable/functional/easy on the eye" or something similar. Respectively, those examples describe the chair's comfort, its utility, and its visual appeal. We are going to go out on a limb here and suggest that you probably haven't managed to completely describe its essence, or really get to the soul of the thing in your one sentence. What we would like you to consider is that if it is hard to do that for a chair, how can we really do it for you? Are you more or less complex than a chair?

Obviously, the judgment *I'm not good enough* hurts, and the perceived solution for experiencing these global negative judgments has been to try and shift toward global positive judgments like *I'm awesome!* In short, the proposed antidote for low self-esteem has been to reach for high self-esteem. Unfortunately, though, research suggests that this has not been a very effective strategy, for reasons we will go into later. While replacing negative judgments with positive affirmations has a few short-term benefits, people often struggle to really believe them, particularly at difficult times when they need them most. It is for this reason that this book is going to take a different tack in terms of how best to respond to negative self-stories and the language of low self-esteem. Instead of talking about reaching for *self-esteem*, we will talk about reaching for *self-acceptance*. We will expand on this throughout the book, although for now, you can think of self-acceptance as seeing your whole self with a greater sense of kindness and compassion, even the bits of you that you don't like so much. We want you to learn to respond to the negative self-stories in a less harsh and critical manner, which is less about trying to get rid of them or block them out and more about letting them in. This might sound counterintuitive. If it does, see if you can make room for any doubt around that just for now. Perhaps, if you've tried to make those stories go away or counter them, and it hasn't worked for you, it might be worth seeing if there is a different way to go about responding to them.

IN SUMMARY

You are amazing, yet a lot of the time, your mind probably comes up with all sorts of reasons why you are not. Problems in the way people see themselves are extremely common among the clients who come to us for help, whether related to self-doubt, a lack of confidence, social anxiety, or thoughts about being worthless. Both of us experience this kind of thing too, and to be honest, we don't know many people who don't to some degree or another. Our view is that this is all about humans being social creatures and that it stems from our need to be part of the group. While this might not help you feel any better in relation to the particular stories your own mind tells you about who you are, sometimes it can help to consider that you are not alone and that you share the human condition with around seven billion others, all of us with our feet on the same ground, all breathing the same air.

Bringing It All Together

Take a moment of reflect on the reasons that you picked up this book. What were you hoping to get out of it? List two or three of the main ones below. This will help you focus on what you want to change over the course of reading the book.

____

____

____

Next, in order to shed some light on what might have influenced the views you have of yourself, try to think about where those reasons came from. For example, do they relate to things you were told as a child or to cultural expectations, or are they based on the story your mind tells you about who you are? Summarize these briefly below.

____

____

____

Lastly, we invite you to reflect upon those reasons now that you have read this chapter. What will you take away from it? Has reading it offered you a different perspective? It may or may not have. Just try to be open and honest with yourself.

____

____

____

CHAPTER 2

How the Self Helps Us and Hurts Us

On the evening before Halloween in 1938, a radio broadcaster interrupted the music show *Ramon Raquello and His Orchestra* to announce that astronomers had observed strange gas explosions coming from Mars. Upon returning to Ramon Raquello and his band, the show was interrupted again with further news bulletins declaring that a strange object had landed in New Jersey. The bulletins went on to announce an alien invasion and an unfolding scene of chaos and destruction around New York City. As implausible as it sounds, panic and mass hysteria among the listening audience ensued as they assumed they were listening to genuine news broadcasts. Of course, what they were listening to was the famous Mercury Theatre adaptation of H. G. Wells's *The War of the Worlds,* produced by the soon-to-be-famous Orson Welles. The hyperrealism, coupled with pre-World War II anxiety, is thought to be part of the explanation for why the audience fell so hard for Mr. Welles's elaborate Halloween prank.

You would be quite reasonable in thinking that this was just an artifact of the times; those gullible old-time folks, there's no way it could ever happen again. And yet, there are at least three documented cases of radio broadcasts, following Welles's format, creating similar, if not worse, chaos and panic. It happened in Santiago, Chile, in 1944; in Quito, Ecuador (with sadly disastrous consequences), in 1949; and again in Buffalo, New York, in 1968 (Bartholomew 2001; Beck 2016; Flynn 2005).

How do we understand this phenomenon? Well, we humans are undoubtedly suckers for a good story. We can become so immersed in narrative stories that we struggle to discern fact from fiction. It's almost like we *want* to believe the stories we hear. Among the stories most compelling to us are the ones we tell about ourselves, and these *self-stories* are immensely helpful in making sense of ourselves, our relationship to other people, and the world we live in. While they can help us to keep ourselves safe (more on this shortly), they can be extraordinarily limiting if we hold on to them too tightly. But understanding your self-story and how it influences your behavior is the first step to overcoming the limits it can place on your life.

WHERE DOES YOUR SENSE OF SELF COME FROM?

The emergence of our sense of self can be traced right back to our arrival as babies into the world. We develop a growing sense of ourselves as a distinct being in a world of other distinct beings and things. Gradually, we learn to use language, which allows us to participate in the verbal community. As we do this, we can more fully interact with ourselves, others, and the world around us—and our self-stories, our stories about others, and our self-esteem emerge.

How Children Learn Who They Are

When we pop out of our moms' tummies and into the world, we make a fairly sharp transition from where we floated blissfully for nine months in a warm bath of amniotic fluid, with our every need taken care of instantaneously. We come into the world kicking and screaming, desperate to be kept warm, dry, and fed. Our only way to communicate our needs is to scream in the hope that someone is listening. And often someone is: your bewildered parents, doing their utmost to stem the tide of tears. But of course, there is no going back. The miraculous process of life drives you to grow and develop as your DNA blueprint interacts with your environment. You start to learn amazing things about who you are and what you can do. For example, you realize that the long sausages that flap about in front of your face are actually your arms, and you can use them to grab at things. As you interact with the world, you come to the slightly unsettling realization that your mother, who you thought was one and the same as you, is actually separate from you. Out of the gloom, a hazy sense of yourself as a distinct being emerges.

As all this happens, your brain is developing at an extraordinary rate, and before you know it, you're using your hands to manipulate the world and your legs to move yourself about in the world. At this point, you are endlessly fascinated by the peculiar noises that those around you make out of their mouths, and you realize you can do the same, sort of. What fun! And so begins your entry into a lifelong love affair with language as the interactive dance between your neural development and your language-rich environment begins.

You begin to figure out that all those noises actually mean something; they are like *symbols* for actual things. You learn that objects around you have names. Even *you* have a name! You learn to relate words to abstract things like thoughts, feelings, wishes, and desires. It slowly dawns on you that you aren't the only one with all this thinking and feeling going on. You develop what experts call a "theory of mind"—an understanding that other people have something similar going on in their minds, too. As this happens, you gain a realization of who you are, as people around you ask questions like "What's your name?" "How tall are you?" "What do you like?" "Why did you do that?" "What do you want to eat today?" All of these questions require an answer, so what do you do? You reach inside and look for an answer. It's expected of us, even from a tender young age, to know ourselves so that we can answer these questions.

As you interact with people around you who ask these questions over and over, you start to develop a sense of yourself that is like an autobiographical story. In early childhood, you probably described yourself in more physical terms, like how big you were, your eye color, and what your favorite food was. As you got older, you became more sophisticated and could describe yourself in terms of more complex internal characteristics, such as feelings, traits, or motivations. The experiences you have as you continue growing up—being raised by your parents, making friends, going to school, getting your first job—gradually furnish you with the details of the story you tell yourself (and others) about who you are: your self-story.

This self can recognize itself in the mirror. It tells you how you are both similar to and distinct from others around you. It gives you a sense of agency over your actions and an appreciation that your thoughts, feelings, and sensations occur from within you. It also acts a bit like a movie director, bringing together your past memories and future plans into a coherent narrative.

Take a moment to describe yourself across the following scenarios, like a movie director would. What do you look like? How do you move? What's your frame of mind?

On a first date?

____

____

____

When pulled over by the police?

____

____

____

Sitting at home on a Sunday in your pajamas?

___

___

___

In a job interview for a position you really, really want?

___

___

___

When someone close to you has deeply let you down?

___

___

___

After one drink too many on a night out?

___

___

___

Notice the similarities and differences across each of these situations. What does this begin to say about the story of who you are? Do any themes emerge? Is there a narrative that surfaces here?

Take some time now to see if you can summarize the themes and narratives that appear. Who are you as a person? What labels do you apply to yourself? How do you describe yourself? We invite you to do this as honestly as possible. It doesn't have to be perfect; just do the best you can.

Here are some responses from people we've worked with when we asked them to describe themselves and their self-story in a nutshell:

"I'm a doormat. I'm weak and pathetic."

"I'm a people pleaser. People like me because I'm so afraid to say no."

"I'm a fraud. On the outside, I'm successful, but underneath I'm a mess."

"I'm a failure. Everything I touch turns to shit."

"I'm broken. There's no way anyone could love me."

Now, take some time to write down your own self-story, in a nutshell:

____

____

____

Throughout this book, we are going to talk a lot about this notion of a self-story, which of course is a metaphor. We don't go around with a T-shirt with the story of ourselves written on the front. Our self-stories tend to be subtle, complex, and often hard to see. They might only be visible in the way we act or treat ourselves and others, or inferred in the things that we do or don't do.

One thing that is true, though, is that we all have one. In case you were harboring the belief that somewhere out there, up in the lofty heights of humanity, there existed the perfect family upbringing, with parents producing the perfect, well-balanced, happy (but not too happy), independent (but of course, not too independent), and strong (but not too strong, we don't want a monster!) children, we have some disappointing news for you. It doesn't exist. The sad reality is that even the most nurturing, warm, and loving parents are going to mess us up to some degree and leave us with unhelpful stories about ourselves that limit what we believe we can do in life. And it's not just our parents who shoulder the responsibility here; it's the rest of our family, teachers, friends, and colleagues—the verbal community in general. They all strongly encourage us to buy in to such a narrative of ourselves.

But why do we let our self-stories limit us so much? Is it that we are irrationally going about sabotaging ourselves and intentionally making our lives more difficult? Well, although they get bad press, it turns out there are often a number of very good reasons why we can cling to our self-stories.

Why We Tell Our Self-Stories

Why is it that we tell ourselves these stories about who we are? First of all, self-stories are great for giving reasons. Why did you say that? Why did you do that? Why do you feel that way? All of these questions demand an answer. When the honest answer is "I really don't know," this feels a little unsatisfactory. We like reasons, explanations, and making sense of things. And these explanations give us a coherent sense of self, which is generally a very useful thing. They help us to provide a sense of order in a chaotic world and to stop us from sliding into a nihilistic black hole. Of course, as we are doing this with ourselves, we are also doing the same with other people, which is to say, we are looking to make sense of others' motives and actions. In this way, we hope to make the complexities of other people just a little bit more predictable.

Our self-stories also work to keep us safe. They become a shorthand way to summarize our past experiences so that we don't end up putting ourselves in painful or difficult situations. For example, if growing up, we experienced others as mean or vindictive, we might reasonably cope with this type of behavior by withdrawing. The trouble comes when eventually it becomes a habit that we do in all social situations, even those that are actually safe. We, or those around us, may conclude that we're shy, and then "I'm shy" becomes our reason for holding back socially—ostensibly to protect ourselves from hurt.

As another example, it may not have been okay in our family to express our needs or to say we were hurt, angry, or upset, because our parents didn't have the capacity to respond to our needs. We might end up developing a pattern of always pushing our needs to one side and over time might conclude, *I'm not important.* This story becomes a way to make sense of our own needs and later in life prevents us from taking risky actions (for example, asking for our needs to be met and risking rejection).

It can be even harder for those of us who have experienced an upbringing far more traumatic than "less than ideal" parenting. Some of us have had childhoods filled with abuse, neglect, violence, and criticism, sometimes to serious or extreme levels. The impact of this is, of course, substantial and long-lasting. As children, we are small, vulnerable, and very much at the mercy, both psychologically and also physically, of the god-like figures who are our parents. Our very survival is at stake, and we therefore do whatever we can to make it through relatively intact. We start to truly believe what we are told about ourselves. We don't question or challenge. We try to make sense of the craziness of being hurt by the very people whose job description is to love and care for us. In these situations, the stories we develop about ourselves are likely to be much more important to our survival in terms of keeping us safe, making sense of what's happening, and helping us understand who we are. Our self-stories become like our anchor in a storm.

Take a moment and think about how your self-story works for you. What function does it serve? Does it keep you safe? Does it help you make sense of other people and your place in the world? Does it tell you who you are? Make some notes about this below.

____

____

____

Of course, your self-story can also become an anchor that keeps you in place and weighs you down. Ruby struggles with a self-story that holds her back from taking actions that would fulfill her. As you read about her, notice the connections between her upbringing, her self-story, and how her self-story works for her.

Ever since she could remember, Ruby's father had been a moderately famous daytime television host. He would invite members of the public onto the show to talk about the various struggles and conflicts in their lives, ostensibly to help, dishing out paternal advice. However, in reality, he was doing it voyeuristically to create sordid drama that brought in the ratings. Ruby found the whole thing excruciating and had been teased mercilessly for it as a kid growing up. Her dad didn't see his job as a problem and had little empathy for his daughter. "Why would you complain so much about what I do? You get everything you want on a silver platter—you're just a useless, pathetic, spoiled brat." After many years of hearing this, Ruby had begun to believe this herself. She didn't have anyone to tell her otherwise. Her mother had disappeared into an alcoholic fog to numb herself from the constant verbal and occasional physical abuse from Ruby's dad, leaving Ruby to be cared for by a steady stream of nannies.

Two failed marriages and a crumbling career as a musician, leaving her dependent on her dad's money, didn't help. She became deeply wedded to the idea that she was a "useless spoiled brat" and would say that to herself in the mirror, especially after heavy cocaine and drinking binges. Her friends could not understand why she would say this about herself. All they saw was a kind, thoughtful, albeit sometimes chaotic, person. Although it sounded incredibly harsh to her friends, Ruby felt oddly better when she said it—the world made a bit more sense and she somehow knew her place. It stopped her from expecting too much of herself and being let down again.

It is easy to see from this how the "useless spoiled brat" story works for both good and ill, and how the combined result of these opposing forces serves to keep Ruby stuck in her current situation.

HOW HAS YOUR SELF-STORY HELD YOU BACK?

Despite all the good reasons we hold on tightly to our self-stories, they can of course be very problematic. Our stories start to limit us; they stop us from doing things that sit outside our narrative. They prevent us from taking risks. They stop us from stepping outside of our comfort zones and trying out new things.

Pause for a moment and take a big, mindful breath. Notice the feeling of the air as it moves out of your nose or lungs. The cool air going in and the warm air out. The sounds of the gentle rustle of nose hairs... Mindful breathing is a wonderful antidote to the busy, mind-filled place of our self-stories. And now, let's dive back in.

What are some of the ways your self-story has held you back in life? Mark any from the list below or add your own:

- ☐ You've held back from telling someone you liked them or loved them.
- ☐ You didn't let someone know when you were hurt by them.
- ☐ You didn't go for that new job or promotion.
- ☐ You've worked too hard to be someone you're not.
- ☐ You haven't allowed yourself to reach for the things in life you've really wanted.
- ☐ You've driven yourself hard and have missed out on important things.
- ☐ You haven't told your friends and family what they mean to you.
- ☐ Others? ____

____

It's hard to pause and think about how life got away from us so that we weren't able to follow our dreams. Hence the mindful breath before this exercise. But well done for picking up this book and listening to your desire to change things for the better. This is where it begins.

To draw this together, we're saying that our self-stories have a helpful side, which explains why we hold on to them so tightly. But they also have an unhelpful side that prevents us from leading a full, rich life of our choosing. The real issue then is not actually the self-story itself. It's your *relationship* to it, which leads us to the next section.

HOW DO YOU RELATE TO YOUR SELF-STORY?

Imagine that your self-story is like a big monster that represents all the things you don't like about yourself. Let's say we take all your negative thoughts, painful emotions, horrible memories, and yucky sensations and cram them under your childhood bed, and out pops a fully formed monster, with horns, sharp teeth, claws, and a tail. On the face of it, this monster is fairly unpleasant, a little scary, and not someone you really want to be associated with. It also leaps up at inconvenient times in your life and likes to tell you how useless you are. It doesn't let you forget all the times you've failed. It likes to remind you how your plans are probably going to go terribly wrong. None of this is particularly nice to listen to, so you end up doing your best to keep it quiet. Perhaps you end up avoiding those times when it gets louder by not challenging yourself or going into new situations. You stick with familiar territory. You play it safe. And overall, this is a successful strategy in that the monster generally keeps quiet.

Very occasionally, you get sick and tired of the monster and you end up yelling back at it. Normally this ends up in a big argument as the monster fires back all the reasons you're wrong. You quietly suspect the monster actually enjoys these arguments.

But the monster has other qualities that get a little obscured by its teeth, claws, and bad breath. For example, its fur is very soft and you like to grab on to it when you're scared. It's big, strong, and authoritative, which makes you feel safe. It's like it knows you well and what you can and can't do, and this is kind of reassuring. It's reliable, predictable, and always on guard for anything that might threaten or challenge you. The world seems a safer, more understandable place when it's lumbering behind you. It's like it's got your back.

Keep in mind, this self-esteem monster is just a metaphor and only one way to look at the issue of self-stories. Other metaphors are of course welcome. We want to emphasize that we're doing this in a respectful way, which is not to minimize or make light of the pain and devastation our stories about ourselves can cause. It's just a way to help create a little space and distance with your self-story to help get your eyes on the qualities of your relationship to it that can easily be obscured.

Let's revisit our example of Ruby. With the help of a therapist, Ruby began to map out her own self-story and her relationship to it. Using the monster metaphor, here's what she said:

> *Well, my monster is definitely big. And he's a he. He stands over me and I feel like I'm in his shadow. He has big meaty fists that he uses to club me down with. He has small, mean, yellow beady eyes that follow me about, judging me. He has sharp teeth that he uses to nip at me, reminding me that I'm good for nothing and I don't deserve anything good to happen to me. This is why I like to drink so much—it gives me a break from him.*

So, in the spirit of being respectfully creative and playful, let's imagine your own self-story comes in the form of a monster. First of all, let's see if we can get an overall sense of what your monster looks like. As you think about all the scary, unpleasant, and nasty thoughts, emotions, memories, and sensations, what comes to mind in terms of your monster? What does it look like? How big is it? What's its body shape? Does it have teeth and claws? Is it a she or a he? Or just an it? What about skin or fur?

____

____

____

____

See if you can let your creative juices flow. It doesn't have to be perfect. Below is how Ruby drew her monster.

Now draw a picture of your monster in the space below.

Now we're going to take some time to reflect on the positive qualities of self-esteem monsters. Let's first see what Ruby said. With some encouragement, Ruby acknowledged some of the positive qualities of her monster:

> *Although he looms over me, his size is weirdly something that's good about him. Like I can't imagine doing life without him. He does overshadow me, but he protects me from doing or saying stupid things, and Lord knows I need help with that. Whenever I have one of my crazy fantasies about making a normal life for myself, he's there to remind me that I'm not that kind of person. I find that comforting. It's like although he's really scary, he has soft, fluffy fur that's nice to cuddle.*

Think for a moment about the positive qualities of your own monster. Does it keep you safe? Does it help you to know your place in the world? Does it help you navigate the complex world of social relationships? Does it tell you important things so you know yourself better? How does your monster help you?

____

____

____

Now see if you can build some of these features into how your monster looks. Does it have big strong muscles? Does it have soft cuddly fur you can bury your face in? Does it look wise and intelligent? Describe these physical features below.

____

____

____

Think also about the kinds of situations where your monster tends to get louder, more aggressive, and more in your face. Then think about the times in which you find yourself turning to it for guidance, reassurance, or support. Write about these situations.

____

____

____

We'd like to invite you to draw your monster again, this time highlighting its positive qualities. Ruby's drawing of her monster is below.

The monster provides a helpful way to look at your self-stories, both the difficult parts and the good parts, how it helps and hinders you. Through this metaphor, something else becomes clearer, which is that there's a *you* that's *separate* from your monster. Sure, it bosses you around a lot. But you don't always listen to it. Again, it's a matter of how you relate to your self-story in any given moment. We'll end this chapter with an exercise to help you see the role and impact of the monster in your life.

NOTICE YOUR MONSTER AT WORK

Over the next few days, see if you can keep track of your monster and watch it at work. The goal is to observe it more consciously. Notice the situations in which it arrives. What parts of it do you see clearly—which thoughts, emotions, associations, memories, and sensations tend to provoke it? How do you respond to it? What do you get from this response? How does this response limit you?

Take a look at Ruby's completed example:

Situation	I got an email from my agent to say a gig got canceled after the venue worried we weren't selling enough tickets.
What does the monster look like?	He was all doom and gloom. He stood over me and told me how useless I was and of course no one really wants to see a tired, old band try and perform.
How did you respond?	I collapsed emotionally inside and felt this massive wave of sadness. I turned off my phone and went straight into bed and tried to go to sleep.
How did your response help?	I felt better, like I could soothe myself and forget all my problems.
How did your response limit you?	It's what I always do. I disconnect from my friends and the world. It doesn't at all help me deal with anything.

Following is a blank worksheet for you to fill in. (You can also download more copies of it at http://www.newharbinger.com/43041.)

Situation	
What does the monster look like?	
How did you respond?	
How did your response help?	
How did your response limit you?	

IN SUMMARY

You've probably worked out by now that we're not going to suggest that the solution here is getting rid of the monster. There are at least two good reasons for this. The first is that it's really hard to just cut out parts of your experience, such as thoughts, emotions, memories, or sensations, especially when they relate to important parts of yourself and your history. We don't come with a convenient delete key on the side of our heads to allow us to get rid of anything we don't like. The second reason is that your self-esteem monster undoubtedly developed for a very good purpose, whether that was to keep you safe, help you make sense of the world, or just tell you who you were. Your history was such that you needed to do whatever it took to make it through and survive. It then makes sense that you cling to those strategies, even though you might recognize how desperately limiting or damaging your relationship with your monster in fact is. So, we need a *brand new* relationship. One that isn't entirely about turning our lives over to the monster, but is not about trying to delete it from our lives either.

In the next chapter, we're going to look at what a new and different relationship with your self-esteem monster could actually be. We're going to introduce you to the concept of self-acceptance, which will help you actively choose how you relate to your monster and move toward building the life you want.

Bringing It All Together

As you pause at the end of this chapter, take a moment to consider this question: what might a different relationship with your monster look like?

____

____

____

What might life look like if your monster weren't constantly blocking the door to the actions you might take? What might you do? Where would you go? Who would you be with?

____

____

____

CHAPTER 3

Moving from Self-Esteem to Self-Acceptance

As we alluded to toward the end of chapter 1, the whole concept of self-esteem rests upon the idea of self-judgment or self-rating. Low self-esteem is a state in which those judgments lie in a negative direction (e.g., *I am unlovable/worthless/a failure*). Those thoughts often come thick and fast, and they can seem pretty compelling and unshakeable. They can show up in all sorts of situations, particularly when facing something new or difficult, and crucially, they can really close down our options in terms of things we choose to do or not do. In the previous chapter, we asked you to think about the ways your negative self-story has held you back at different points in your life. Considering all of our missed opportunities can be a very painful realization. And all of it happened because we believed our minds. It can also be quite sobering to realize that you no longer own that story of yours, and that it has started to own you.

HOW WE TRY TO CHANGE OUR STORIES

Quite understandably, lots of approaches to low self-esteem take the view that the antidote to having to listen to all of those negative and critical things your mind says to you about who you are is to replace them with positive things. They suggest that we reexamine all the judgments we make about ourselves and attempt to push them in an upward direction. That we simply hold ourselves in high regard by listening to and emphasizing the positive voices that *also* sound in our heads from time to time. For a long time, this was seen by mainstream psychology as the answer to the problem of low self-esteem.

Before we explain why this approach doesn't work, try out the activity below to see if there are any different or opposing self-stories that compete for your attention.

THE DIFFERENT STORIES IN OUR HEADS

Take a moment to consider the different things your mind says to you about who you are. Often the easier part of this task is to tune in to the critical stuff. There may be many negative self-stories, but see if you can pick the three most dominant ones and write them below.

I am ____.

I am ____.

I am ____.

Now see if there is anything different or contradictory that ever makes itself known. What positive or encouraging things do you notice your mind saying? Make a list of the three most obvious ones below. If you find this difficult and you can't come up with anything, that's okay. If it is easier, write down some positive things that other people might say about you if we asked them to complete this task.

I am ____.

I am ____.

I am ____.

The positive and the negative self-stories that show up in our minds are something like those old cartoons depicting Donald Duck with a little angel on one shoulder and a devil on the other. Both occupy their own spot and try and influence Donald's behavior in different directions. Perhaps you could imagine your own personalized version of this with your low self-esteem monster on one shoulder and something that represents that kinder, more generous voice on the other. This image reflects your ability to notice both narratives and make some choices about which one to attend to, although there are different ways to proceed with noticing and choosing.

The quest for high self-esteem usually involves a strategy that is all about striving to feed the angel and quiet the devil. It is as if we could achieve a state whereby the angel's voice is all that we hear, and the devil is relegated to the background. Sounds pretty appealing. It would be great if we never ever heard the bad stuff, or, if we did, we could just drown it out with the good stuff: out with the self-doubt, and in with confidence. The trouble is—and you may already know this if you have tried to somehow *talk* yourself into feeling good—this strategy doesn't really work, or if it does, it's very fleeting, since the devil's voice is too loud and compelling to ignore for long.

THE PROBLEM WITH SELF-ESTEEM

Life is hard work. Stress and adversity are just part of the deal, and there is no healthy way of inoculating yourself against the experience of difficult thoughts and feelings. Difficult events, negative thoughts, and worrying that you are not good enough at some aspect of life are pretty much inevitable. There really is no healthy way of "quieting the devil" on your shoulder. Think about this for a moment. You have probably tried a few other things to deal with your low self-esteem monster before picking up this book. Think about all the ways you have tried to escape your negative self-story. How did they work out for you? Did they make it go away? Did you defeat the monster? Did the fight against it cost you anything? Complete the activity below to get to the heart of this.

MY FIGHT WITH MY MONSTER

What have you tried in the service of overcoming low self-esteem?

____

____

____

____

How did these things work out in the short term?

____

____

____

____

____

How did they work out in the long term?

____

____

____

____

____

Did you win the fight? Did the monster disappear for good?

____

____

____

Did the fight cost you anything or have any unintended consequences?

____

____

____

If you have hit upon a really great strategy that helps you deal effectively with your negative self-story that you can use repeatedly at no cost to you or those around you, then we would encourage you to do more of that. In fact, you should probably not waste your time reading on. Put the book in the trash and go out and live your life!

WHAT YOU RESIST PERSISTS

Still here? Yeah, so are we. You can't feel better about yourself by force. Trying to "win" the battle with the monster and replace low self-esteem with high self-esteem does not have a good track record. In fact, in a huge review of more 20,000 research studies into self-esteem interventions, the authors concluded, "We have not found evidence that boosting self-esteem causes benefits" (Baumeister et al. 2003, 1). Well, that's a cruel blow, right?! Not what you wanted to read? So much for trying to raise self-esteem. So, why doesn't it work? Here are a few potential answers to that question. First, attempting to quiet the monster implies that what it says is intrinsically bad. If you adopt the attitude that you simply cannot have the bad stuff that it says you have, something paradoxical will happen: you will give it loads of attention in the service of getting rid of it. Rather than quiet it, this usually amplifies it since you will listen for it, tune in to it, and then try to erase it. This leads to a constant fight that you can never win because negative events are inevitable, and so are uncomfortable thoughts and distressing emotions. Also, you can't change the past experiences that have contributed to your self-story and the way you currently feel.

It's a bit like actively trying to avoid something ubiquitous and naturally occurring, like birds. You could go to a great deal of trouble to confine yourself to places where birds don't normally hang out, although in doing so you would need to find out about their habits and learn how best to avoid them. You could monitor your strategy to see how well it is working, which would require turning your bird radar up to maximum. In time, you would develop a finely tuned sense of birds' whereabouts and an encyclopedic knowledge of everything to do with them. And how is that avoiding them? What you would have done is brought birds front and center in your awareness, and they would have come to dominate your every move. In the same way, trying to deny the presence of your self-story feels like a rigged game that you can never really win.

Second, trying to exclusively buy in to the good stuff can function like a short-term trap. Artificially inflating our self-esteem by just focusing on our good qualities or avoiding thinking about the less desirable ones can work temporarily. We can get a boost that might keep us coming back for more of the same. Most of us are attracted by "smaller sooner" kinds of rewards (waiting for "larger later" is usually more effortful since it involves having to delay our gratification). However, while temporary short-term boosts can work for a while if everything is going okay around you, they often don't last due to the inevitability of negative events, uncomfortable thoughts, and distressing emotions. It's easy to feel good about yourself when things are going well...and it's much more difficult when they aren't. Self-esteem ratings are often related to a particular attribute or event (e.g., *I failed my exam—I am a failure)* and set us up for the short-term trap. If you boost yourself with *I'm a success,* that isn't going to serve you very well when you eventually do fail that exam. We are inherently fallible as human beings. With the best will in the world, each and every one of us will screw up at some point or another. If you pretend to yourself that you are somehow immune from adversity or failure, aside from the potential for fueling some kind of narcissism, it's going to hit you pretty hard when it arrives, frequently leaving you feeling like a fraud.

Related to the above issue is the problem that self-esteem can involve an unnecessary rating. "I failed my exam; therefore I am a failure" involves a second rating that probably isn't helpful and doesn't really make sense. Does failing an exam really make you "a failure" in totality? Wouldn't you be better off just stopping after the first rating and acknowledging that you could have done better on the exam? The quest for high self-esteem always seems to depend on things going well. We feel good about ourselves when we believe we are succeeding in things that we think (or are told) are important. Conversely, we feel bad about ourselves when we believe we have failed to live up to our ideal in those same things. To cut a long story short, constantly reaching for that feel-good, high self-esteem story leaves us very fragile. Thankfully, there is a different way to approach the devil on our shoulder: self-acceptance.

WHAT IS SELF-ACCEPTANCE?

Self-acceptance, in this context, is the ability to see yourself, in all your complexity, with kindness and compassion. It includes seeing your inadequacy and pain as just another part of your experience. It's tempting to see your negative self-story, or your monster, as a problem that needs to be solved, but what if it's just evidence that you're a fallible human being like everybody else?

With self-acceptance, your regard for yourself is not based on how things are going, what others think, or your sense of whether you've succeeded or failed. Our contention here is quite a big one and involves getting a little philosophical for a second. Here it comes...

> *All human beings are of equal worth, irrespective of what they have achieved or done or what is happening around them.*

Let's really stop and think about this. Is your worth as a person enhanced if you perform well at something? Does it make you a better person than someone who performs less well? Is your worth as a person diminished if you perform badly at something? Would you raise a child to believe that their worth wholly depends on being good at stuff? It is somewhat uncomfortable to note that this is often what happens, albeit subtly, when a child's good action is rewarded with "Good girl/boy!" and undesirable behavior is met with "Bad girl/boy!" The rating game of global self-evaluation is supported by this kind of language, and the impact over time of hearing these messages is the belief that your worth depends on your actions. Our view is that this is not a helpful way to see yourself or your fellow humans. Indeed, while it is often helpful to have feedback on aspects of our behavior (for example, we would welcome you leaving us a book review on Amazon!), it is hard to think of a situation where a global judgment is really helpful. Neither "You are a complete idiot!" nor "You are totally awesome!" is a particularly constructive bit of feedback. When we said you are amazing, back in chapter 1, we were referring to your incredible complexity, and that includes the good bits *and* those bits that you're not so content with.

To consider this idea from a different perspective, what would you look for in a close friend or confidante? What qualities would you like them to possess? Take a few minutes to think about this and make some notes below.

Obviously, it's impossible for us to know what you just wrote down…and we are sitting here wondering anyway. We are willing to bet that your closest and most valuable friends are the ones you can laugh *and* cry with.

What is it that attracts you to another person? Would you be attracted to someone who is genuine, authentic, and honest about their mix of good, bad, and indifferent qualities, or someone who is unerringly positive and only ever reveals the good things about themselves? As strange as it might sound, many of us are attracted by the vulnerabilities that others display, and it is well known that qualities like empathy and vulnerability drive connection between people. As suggested by researcher and TED-talker Brené Brown, a willingness to be vulnerable is one of the *last* things we want to demonstrate and one of the *first* things we look for in someone else (Brown 2012). Everyone has good, bad, and neutral qualities, and we cannot fully describe anyone with just a single judgment. People are constantly changing and developing; they have the ability to make mistakes and to learn from them. They are not defined just by their behavior or achievements. Are you able to accept others in all their complexity? Can you see that they are human, worthy simply for who they are? Could you learn to see yourself this way too? The exercise below asks you to take a broad view of another person, taking in a range of qualities, both desirable and otherwise.

I SEE YOU, AND SEE YOU SEEING ME

Think of someone you know whom you trust. Someone who you know also trusts you and has really got your back. Bring to mind their face and imagine them looking back at you. If you have a picture of them, it might help to look at it. If they are with you, you could even invite them to do this exercise with you. Simply focus your mind on the person's face and consider the statements and questions below. Take a mindful pause between questions to consider your answer to each one, noticing any thoughts and feelings that show up around your answers.

Notice this perfectly formed human being in front of you. Realize that being a human being means that they cry and that they have hopes, dreams, and struggles, just like you. They experience joy, sadness, anxiety, anger, and disgust. They hurt, they care, they succeed, and they screw up, just like you.

What if, within this person's history, there was something that might be uncomfortable for you to know. Would you still be able to trust them? Would you still reach out and help them if they needed it?

If you would still be able to trust them, could you consider that they might still be able to trust you too if there were something in your history that they found difficult?

What if you could see right through this person, through their roles, their self-stories, and the fronts they put up? What if you could see right into the suffering they experience with the things that they find difficult? Would you still be able to accept them as they are?

If you would still be able to accept them, could you consider that they might still be able to accept you too?

Sometimes this person needs help and sometimes this person is the one that does the helping. Can you feel kindness for them with respect to both of those roles?

If you would be able to feel kindness for them, could you consider that they might be able to feel kindness for you too?

Finally, what would need to change about this person in order for you to accept them as a whole, complete human being?

If you would be able to accept them as a whole, complete human being, could you consider that they might be able to accept you too?

What was it like to think about taking an accepting and compassionate stance toward someone else, even while thinking about parts of their history or character that might be more difficult? Sometimes this is easier to do with respect to another person and harder to do with ourselves. This is the essence of self-acceptance.

MOVING TOWARD SELF-ACCEPTANCE

You probably know uncomfortable thoughts and feelings well. You have probably spent a lot of time trying to get rid of them and maybe have thought that life will be better once they are all gone. From a place of self-acceptance, we are asking you to consider that these experiences are only a *part* of you. We'll cover this more later, but first, let's consider a few assumptions about humanity that are involved in self-acceptance. You may not agree with them, and that's okay.

Each human being on our planet is:

- composed of good, bad, and indifferent qualities
- too complex to be described by a single judgment, such as "worthless" (although it may be workable to rate aspects of people so they can take credit for positive qualities or address less desirable ones)

- always changing and developing
- fallible (i.e., has an incurable tendency to make mistakes)
- equal to others in terms of intrinsic worth and a shared humanity, even if different in specific ways (such as skin color, gender, height, or academic ability)
- not defined by their behavior
- unique—just like all the others!

Self-acceptance involves extending kindness and compassion to oneself, especially during times of perceived inadequacy, seeing this as just another part of your experience. Unlike the idea of self-esteem, it provides more stability since it is not based on how well external things are going or what others think. It is not based on perceptions of passing successes or failures, but rather upon a value of how we might aspire to treat ourselves and each other. Self-acceptance is useful precisely when the search for self-esteem fails: when we are suffering or feel we are failing in some way.

Life is frequently difficult and demanding. In fact, most of us have a history that contains a lot of adversity and possibly even traumatic memories. A lot of our current stresses are reflections of this. If you experience thoughts about not being good enough, there is a good chance that they are echoes of your history, ringing around in your present. It is tempting to see the presence of such thoughts and judgments as a problem that needs solving. But is it really a problem? Does it really need solving? A self-accepting view is that your difficult thoughts and feelings are not the enemy and that their presence doesn't prove anything bad about you. All it proves is your human fallibility and maybe that you've been through some tough times.

IN SUMMARY

The traditional way to approach the thoughts associated with low self-esteem has been to work toward high self-esteem, which, as you have seen, doesn't work so well. Alternatively, you can choose to approach those thoughts with an attitude of self-acceptance. Self-acceptance involves taking a broader view of ourselves and working toward a kinder, more compassionate position in which we accept the difficult parts of our history and our current experience. Rather than fighting your monster in a desperate attempt to feel good all the time, you can choose to make room for it, accept that it's there, and move on to taking *action* in the direction that you want your life to go. There is a lot of evidence to suggest that self-acceptance has a better chance of working out. In the next chapter, we'll introduce you to a tool, the matrix, that will help you learn how to practice self-acceptance.

Bringing It All Together

Take a brief pause to consider what you have taken from this chapter. What has resonated with you regarding the differences between self-esteem and self-acceptance?

____

____

____

Applying these ideas to your own life, can you think of any reasons why adopting a more self-accepting stance would be helpful to you? What, if any, difference might it make?

____

____

____

Lastly, what reservations do you have? Maybe the low self-esteem monster is acting up and raising all sorts of objections to the notion of self-acceptance. If that's the case, it would be good to note those down here too.

____

____

____

CHAPTER 4

The Matrix: A Tool for Making Sense of the Self

We can overcome limits placed on us by low self-esteem, and better practice self-acceptance, if we come to understand what's motivating our response in a given moment. The matrix (Polk et al. 2016) is a tool that can help us do this, and in this chapter we'll learn how. Derived from acceptance and commitment therapy (ACT), the matrix is a method of mapping the way you're reacting to the things you encounter and understanding how you could respond differently so as to move closer to your values, rather than just away from what you fear and what makes you feel bad.

AUTOPILOT AND AWARENESS MODES

At the heart of being human is doing, taking actions, and behaving. We are constantly talking, moving, eating, hugging, writing, or thinking. Even when we're sitting absolutely still and not moving, we're still behaving.

If you're like most people on the planet, there's a good chance that a large proportion of this behavior is pretty unconscious. That is to say that it's a product of habits and routines that were established a long time ago. Have you ever had that experience of brushing your teeth without really thinking about how you did it? Or driving down the highway and suddenly realizing you have no recollection of the last half hour of driving? That's your *autopilot mode* doing its thing. This is not as bad as it might sound. It means we don't need to be a micromanager, constantly checking and making sure everything is running as it should. We can let the autopilot take over and do the job for us, giving us more time to think about the important things in life. Or it's when we let our self-esteem story make the decisions for us. Someone compliments us, and we immediately respond by saying they didn't really mean it. An opportunity comes our way, and we turn it down without thinking because we know there's no way we could manage.

The other mode is when we do things with more awareness. For example, remember when you *learned* to drive? Hyperconscious, grinding gears, oversteering to avoid oncoming traffic, while shaving years off your poor driving instructor's life? Or when you did something meaningful like listen to your favorite band live or hold a baby for the first time? Or the odd occasion you took a risk and stepped outside your comfort zone, even though your self-esteem story told you it was all going to go horribly, terribly wrong? These are all examples of being in the awareness mode. In this mode, we are more attentive to the present moment—to what's going on around us and inside of us—and to the consequences of our actions.

Understanding the distinction between autopilot and awareness modes is particularly helpful for working with self-esteem self-stories—especially the unpleasant, unwanted ones that become monster-like—which is where responding on autopilot is very easy to do, *and* can get us into trouble.

The degree to which what we're thinking and feeling is unpleasant and unwanted also has a hold on us in another sense: it can dictate whether we move *toward* an experience we're having or an action we're taking or *away* from it.

MOVING TOWARD AND MOVING AWAY

Pause for a second and imagine you're walking through the forest at the end of a long day of hiking. You've covered many miles and seen some amazing sights. Now, as you notice that your feet are sore and you're feeling tired, you come to a fork in the trail. You stop for a moment to decide which side of the fork to go down. To help make up your mind, you check them both out first.

At the end of one path, you see an orchard of apple trees bathed in sunshine. You notice that the trees are laden with big, fat, juicy apples, and your stomach growls with hunger. Apples are a tasty and healthy snack, you think to yourself.

You also look down the other path in the fork, just to see what's there. And through the dark undergrowth, you hear another growl. This time it's definitely not your stomach, but much louder and threatening. You see a rather large grizzly bear glaring at you with its claws and teeth at the ready!

So, which path do you take? This is not a trick question. Apples are tasty and healthy. Grizzly bears are less good for you, and you remember vividly what happened to Leonardo DiCaprio's character, Hugh Glass, after his encounter with one in *The Revenant*. Not good for Hugh. Quite naturally, you take the path toward the apples. And that's how most of us work most of the time; we move *toward* the stuff in life that we like or enjoy or that makes us feel good, and we move *away* from the things that scare us or make us feel unhappy.

But of course, we're not just a simple amoeba bouncing around in a primordial soup, instinctively swimming toward warm, happy nutrients and away from toxic pools or larger, unfriendly amoebas. We are complex, made much more so by our ability to use language to think, reason, and make meaning. Through language, we apply the same rules we used for apples and bears to thoughts, feelings, and emotions, treating them the same. We move toward the ones we like, and we move swiftly away from the ones we don't like, responding to them as if they could do us actual harm, like a grizzly could. Although on the surface this may appear logical, it has a significant drawback.

To illustrate this, take a moment to think about something you've achieved in life that you feel a little bit proud of. It could be a project or study you completed or a relationship goal you achieved. It doesn't have to be big, just something where at the end you felt a little flutter of pride. Write the achievement down here.

____

____

Now, think back to the moment just before you embarked on your journey toward the goal. See if you can take yourself right back to the moment. What emotions were present?

____

____

____

We're willing to bet that you felt a range of emotions. Perhaps some nice ones, such as excitement at the prospect of achieving the goal...and probably some less comfortable ones, such as anxiety (*What if it all goes wrong?*), doubt (*I don't know if I've got what it takes*), or dread (*I'm going to screw it up like last time!*). In spite of these, you persisted and completed the goal. Well done. You made the distinction between an emotion related to something that could definitely harm you (like the fear when you encounter a big grizzly) and an emotion related to scenarios your mind produced. And once you made that distinction, you made a decision to take steps toward your goal and ultimately achieve it.

But we're also willing to bet that, like every other person on the planet, you've experienced times when you've thought about setting a personal goal, and anxiety, doubt, and fear naturally arose, but your self-esteem monster got the better of you and talked you out of it. Take a moment to reflect on such an instance and write down what the goal was, what feelings came up, and what your monster said to talk you out of it.

____

____

____

____

____

Finally, think about what your monster was trying to protect you from. Put a check mark next to any reasons from the list below or add your own:

- ☐ You'll fail like you did before (protection from feelings of failure).
- ☐ You won't be able to stand the feelings; it'll be too much (protection from painful feelings).
- ☐ You don't have what it takes; you're not that kind of person (protection of your sense of self).
- ☐ Everyone will laugh at you (protection from rejection or ridicule).
- ☐ You don't have enough time, money, or energy (protection from wasting resources).
- ☐ Others? _______________________________________

  ____

Now, some of these reasons may have some truth to them depending on the situation. Maybe you really weren't ready to give that presentation at work that you decided not to give; maybe you really would've been judged at that party you decided not to go to. But our point is that self-esteem monsters will *always* come up with reasons, excuses, or justifications whenever we look to step outside of our comfort zone. They'd prefer us to stay at home on the couch watching TV with them, missing out on life.

If you were a person who *never* left their comfort zone when feelings like this showed up, you would be very comfortable all the time (sort of), but you'd never get to experience the thrill and joy of moving toward the things in life that matter to you.

This is a key point to take home from this chapter: we can broadly organize our behavior to move toward the things in life that matter to us (for example, our important relationships and meaningful activities) and use these as a guide for our behavior. Or, we can broadly organize our behavior so that it is largely driven by our self-esteem stories ("I can't do it," "I'm not enough," "I don't have what it takes") and move away from things that scare us or that we don't like (such as painful thoughts, feelings, or memories)—things that make us uncomfortable but can't actually harm us.

The big risk in employing only the second strategy is that it can be very limiting and you don't get the opportunity to build the life you want. Sure, it might be safer, but it won't be very meaningful. It won't be the kind of life you care about.

This book is about helping you choose the kind of life that you really care about and take action to move toward that life, *even when* these actions trigger your self-esteem stories. The matrix is a tool that can put you in charge of your choices, as opposed to being at the mercy of your low self-esteem.

INTRODUCING THE MATRIX

If you are hoping Keanu Reeves is going to show up, we're sorry to disappoint you. Still, the matrix is pretty cool.

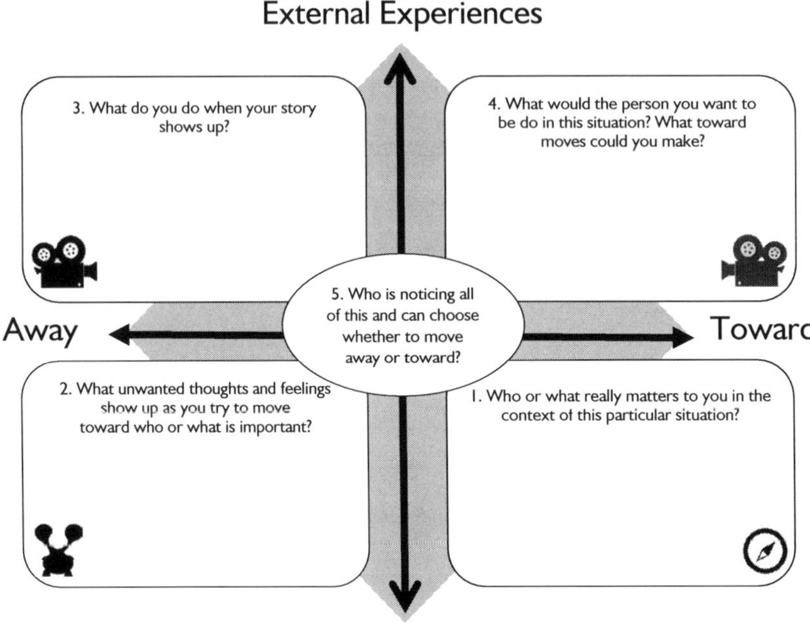

As you can see on the diagram, the matrix is made up of four quadrants. The horizontal line going through the middle represents moving toward and moving away. Everything below that line is an internal experience that other people wouldn't know about unless you told them (e.g., thoughts and feelings), whereas everything above the line is an external experience, or an observable behavior. You can see that in each of the quadrants there is a question. Together, these questions give us a way to map out, in the moment, our values and what gets in the way of living in accordance with our values, for example, our self-esteem stories or the fear and panic that we can feel in the moments that we're challenged. This helps us to spot whether, in any given moment, we're acting to move away from something we don't want to feel or experience or acting to get more of what we do want.

Who or What Is Important in Life?

Quadrant 1 (bottom right) refers to the things that matter to you in life. The question there is, who or what matters? What does your heart cry out for? Where are the places in life that you feel most vital, alive, and engaged? There are four domains that people tend to talk about:

Love—relationships (friends, family, intimate partners; your relationship with yourself)

Work—meaningful activity, contributing, learning, or studying

Health—physical and mental health, well-being

Play—downtime, fun and creativity

You will also see a little compass symbol in this quadrant. This is to remind you that our values are like a compass; they provide a direction to head in to move toward that value.

What Shows Up and Gets in the Way?

Life is not a four-lane highway heading off into the sunset. It's not enough to just identify what's important; we also have to contend with all the painful, unwanted, and difficult thoughts, emotions, associations, memories, and sensations (for which we use the nifty acronym TEAMS) that show up as we live life and especially when we move toward who or what's important (or even just think about it!). These TEAMS are represented by the little monster symbol in this quadrant. This is perhaps a little odd to say, but in fact, this is the stuff of life: the things that show up when we contemplate moving toward what matters. This is the focus of quadrant 2 (bottom left). It's also the part of the matrix where the self-esteem monsters tend to hang around.

What Do You Do When Your Story Shows Up?

Here, we are looking at all the actions or behaviors that we do to try and either quiet our monsters or run away from them. This is quadrant 3 (top left) of the matrix. You can see a little camera there; this is to remind you that we're looking for all the behaviors and actions we can see, or capture on a video camera. Here's a list of some of our personal favorites:

- Excessively and obsessively planning
- Netflix bingeing
- Procrastinating
- Not being honest with other people or ourselves
- Avoiding difficult or challenging situations
- Staying in bed
- Eating too much

- Eating too little
- Trying to control ourselves, other people, or life in general
- Using alcohol
- Putting ourselves down
- Putting other people down
- Ignoring our own needs
- Being excessively compliant and "nice"

Of course, this is by no means an exhaustive list. You'll get a chance later in the chapter to identify your own top strategies.

How Can You Move Toward What Matters to You?

In quadrant 1, we asked you to take out your "what matters" compass and consider who or what is important; just like a compass, your values are like a guide to action. Quadrant 4 (top right) asks about what actual, concrete actions you would want to take to move you in the direction of who or what is important. What actions you would take if your values or the things that matter to you were prominent? What would the person you want to be do in this situation? What moves could you make *toward* the things that are important to you? You can see in the diagram that we've drawn another camera to remind you that this is about actions—things you do, rather than feelings or thoughts. We emphasize this because we have more say about our actions; thoughts and feelings are generally a lot less in our control.

Who Is Noticing All This?

The last question takes us to the center of the matrix: Who is noticing all these thoughts, emotions, associations, memories, sensations (remember, TEAMS), and behaviors? The answer of course is you. You are the one who has the capacity to notice this stuff. Your monster can show up and boss you around, but it's just one part of you. And even as you're obeying the monster, there is another, larger part of you that observes, notices, and watches all of this. And it's from that observing place that you get to *legitimately* choose the action you want to take, rather than your monster doing the choosing for you—once you learn to flexibly shift perspective in the moments that your monster and your self-esteem stories get really loud.

COLLETTE'S STORY

Collette works as a teacher in a busy urban school. Although she loved teaching, she found working with her colleagues difficult as she had a constant nagging fear that they were better teachers than she was. She found it extremely difficult to say no to any requests from other teachers and especially the principle. She felt that saying no would expose her as not as competent as her peers. As a result, last year, she ended up taking on lots of extracurricular activities, which eventually led to her burning out. She had to take three months off work to deal with all the stress and anxiety that had built up.

Now, as she returned to work, Collette was plagued with self-doubt, worried she didn't have what it took to do her job. The volume on her self-esteem monster was turned up to maximum:

"You're incompetent and stupid."

"Everyone else is so together."

"They can see how useless you are."

"You're so pathetic for even thinking this."

Collette was clearly struggling with her self-esteem. This was heightened as she had a school board meeting coming up where she had been asked to do a presentation about the future direction of the school. Her self-esteem monster of course cranked the volume up even higher. At this point, she realized she needed help, and, following a recommendation from a good friend, she decided to see a therapist.

In their first meeting, Collette told her therapist about what had been going on. She had never really told anyone else about her low self-esteem and the things her mind said to her, but her therapist was warm and kind and Collette felt she could trust her. The therapist suggested they complete a matrix together to help make sense of what was happening. This would enable Collette to put her self-story aside for a while to figure out what she might do.

Let's go through each quadrant together, one at a time, and follow Collette as she goes through her own matrix.

Who or What Is Important in Life?

The therapist explored the question posed in quadrant 1.

Therapist: I know the prospect of the upcoming presentation is quite stressful, but let me ask perhaps a slightly counterintuitive question. In doing this talk, what, if anything, is important about it?

Collette: I'm not sure I get what you mean. It's just stressful and I don't want to do it!

Therapist: I guess that's why I said it was a bit of a counterintuitive question. Often, when things are stressful, most of us don't tend to pause and think about whether it represents a chance to express what matters to us.

Collette: Ah, okay, I think I know what you mean. Well, I'd really like to push the school board to upgrade our computers for the kids. It's such a hinderance teaching them on slow and outdated systems. I want them to be properly prepared!

Therapist: Okay, so I hear something important here. Even though it's stressful and pushes your buttons, this could be about something that really matters to you.

Collette: Yeah, you're right. Properly preparing my students is *really* important to me.

What Shows Up and Gets in the Way?

To explore quadrant 2, Collette's therapist presented the concept of self-esteem monsters and then explored what shows up for Collette in terms of her self-esteem story as she thinks about what's important.

Therapist: Okay, so knowing self-esteem monsters as I do, I bet it gets loud as you think about this, particularly when you identify what's important.

Collette: Oh yes! It's telling me I'm a joke, I'm stupid, no one is going to be interested in my silly little ideas.

Therapist: Yowch. It doesn't pull its punches then. How are you feeling in your body when this is going on?

Collette: I feel like I've been kicked in the guts.

What Do You Do When Your Story Shows Up?

Collette's response to the therapist's last question led smoothly to a discussion of quadrant 3.

Therapist: So, when your monster has completely caught your attention, what do you tend to do?

Collette: Well, I do two things. I work extra hard and take on more work so I can be sure that people think I'm a hard worker, or at least not completely useless. You wouldn't believe how many hours I've spent on this presentation already. The other thing I do is criticize myself, like really badly. I feel like I deserve it. And I also worry that if I don't, I'll just slack off.

Therapist: And how do those strategies work for you? Short term? Long term?

Collette: This may sound a little weird, but they both work well. I get stuff done, and when I give myself a hard time, I get motivated.

Therapist: Yeah, I get that. What about long term?

Collette: Well, my monster is still very much part of my life. And I feel pretty shitty about myself. Worse actually, over the years.

How Can You Move Toward What Matters to You?

At this point, the therapist shifted the discussion to quadrant 4.

Therapist: So, if you were letting the things that matter guide your actions here, what would you do?

Collette: Well, I'd not freak out and make this into a huge deal.

Therapist: (*noticing that Collette is talking about her feelings*) If this is more about acting as the kind of person you'd want to be, what would I see you do?

Collette: Okay, so, I'd probably be nervous—I hate presenting. But I'd find a way to make it engaging and interesting. The board members are generally enthusiastic about tech and see it as a good investment for the school. I think I have a good shot at swaying them.

Therapist: Okay, nice. I see you light up a little as you describe that. What else?

Collette: Well, I probably wouldn't push myself for weeks beforehand trying to prepare it perfectly just so I could be sure everyone loved it. I'd focus on good enough and not give myself such a hard time.

Together with her therapist, Collette used the matrix to tease apart her feelings and the actions connected with avoiding those feelings. Collette's therapist also helped her move her focus away from her stress and fears that she won't do a good job and on to actions she might take, as well as her values that drive these actions. Collette is now in a much better position to approach the presentation with her values guiding her and engage in it in a more meaningful way.

USING THE MATRIX

Okay, this is your chance to practice. We'd like you to complete a matrix for yourself. As you practice, keep in mind, it doesn't have to be exactly right. Find a quiet moment, sit down with a cup of coffee or tea, and fill in a matrix form (which you can download at http://www.newharbinger.com/43041).

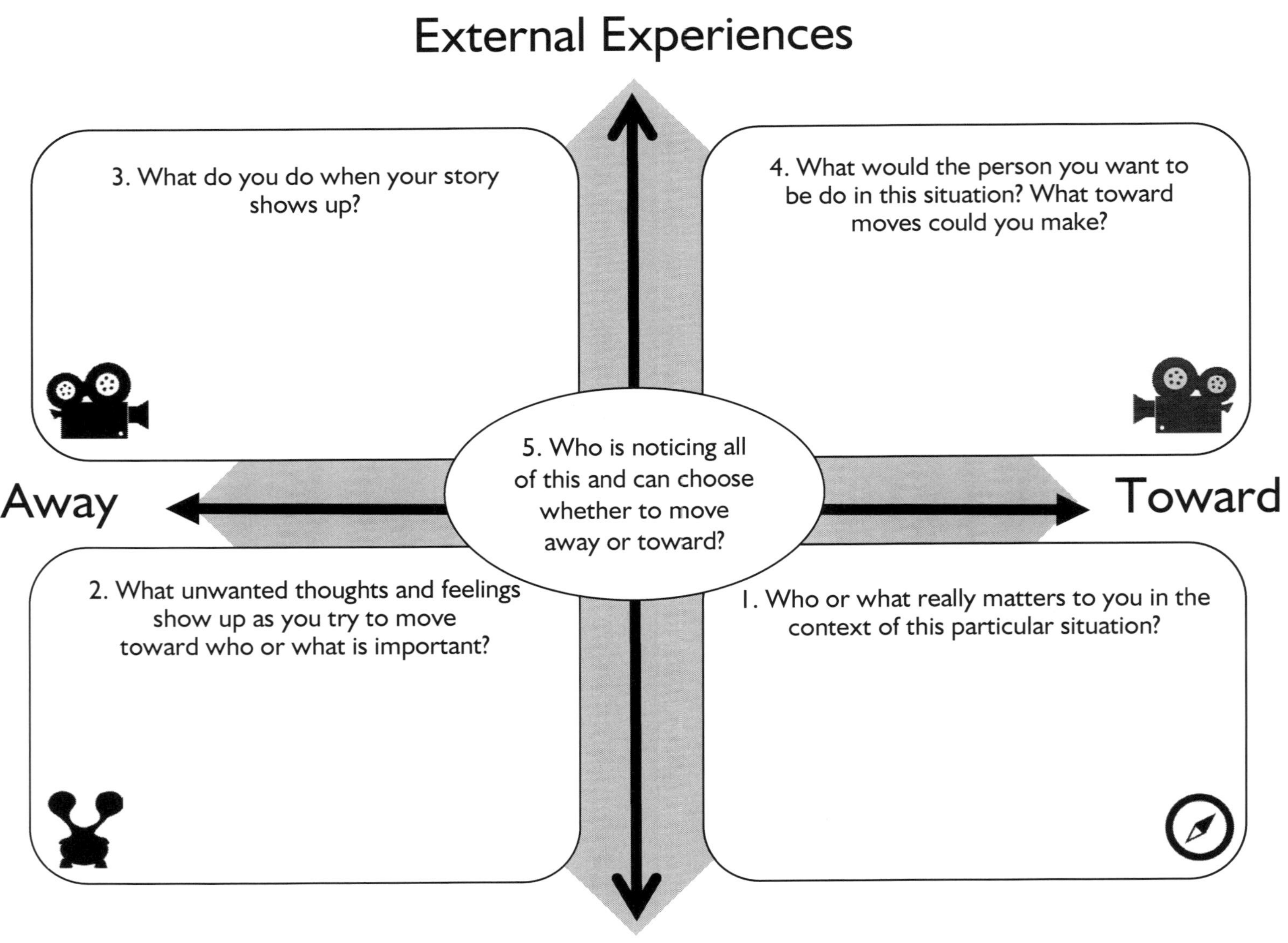
External Experiences
3. What do you do when your story shows up?
4. What would the person you want to be do in this situation? What toward moves could you make?
Away
5. Who is noticing all of this and can choose whether to move away or toward?
Toward
2. What unwanted thoughts and feelings show up as you try to move toward who or what is important?
1. Who or what really matters to you in the context of this particular situation?
Internal Experiences

Who or What Is Important in Life?

Think about a particular situation that is causing you difficulty at the moment because your self-story is getting in the way—the "I'm not good enough" or "I can't do this" stories are too loud and hard to get around. Now take a moment to fill in quadrant 1 in relation to this situation, answering the question "Who or what is important to you?" If this situation spoke to what mattered to you deep down, what would it say about what is important to you?

What Shows Up and Gets in the Way?

In quadrant 2, write down the stuff that gets in the way in this situation. This includes your self-stories and any painful or difficult feelings (your TEAMS).

What Do You Do When Your Story Shows Up?

So what kinds of things do you do when you're trying to either quiet down your monster or get away from it? In quadrant 3, make a list of all those actions that are designed to pull you away from or make you try to avoid pursuing the things you care about. You might want to look back at the list in the section "What Do You Do When Your Story Shows Up?" for ideas.

Some of these actions might be helpful, and some are likely to be very unhelpful. Don't worry too much about that for now. The idea is just to list all the things you do that are about moving away from painful self-stories, even if it's at the expense of your happiness. After you've completed your list, make a note as to how well each response works. In the short term, does it help you deal with the painful thoughts, feelings, and self-esteem stories? How about in the longer term?

How Can You Move Toward What Matters to You?

Remember, quadrant 4 asks about what actual, concrete actions you would want to take to move you in the direction of who or what is important—to follow your compass. Now fill in this final quadrant, answering the question in relation to the situation: if you were able to act as the person you would choose to be and be guided by your values, what actions would you take?

Knitting Your Matrix Together

Let's take some time now to knit each of the quadrants together and see how they're connected and influence each other. You can perhaps now see how there are broadly two potential guides for your actions and behavior.

THE AWAY MOVES

The first guide is the old and familiar, which is the left side of the matrix and away from what's important. Here, the driver for your actions is your monster *and* your relationship with it. In other words, when it's captured your attention and you're fully focused on it, are you doing your best to listen to it or keep it quiet?

We invite you to bring less *automaticity* to your actions so you get to really choose. Here are some questions to consider in regard to your away moves:

Have the actions you've taken to deal with your self-esteem stories (which you wrote down in quadrant 3 of your matrix) helped to solve your problems in the long term? Make a few notes about this.

____

____

____

Have your away moves—those things you do when you're trying to avoid taking a risk in order to act on something you care about—helped you to move toward who or what's important? If so, how? If not, why?

____

____

____

How does moving away from pain and unpleasantness get in the way of moving toward what you care about?

____

____

____

THE TOWARD MOVES

The other guide is, of course, your values compass. You can at any point pause proceedings, metaphorically whip your compass out, and ask yourself, *In this moment, if I could take action to be the person I'd choose to be, what would I do?* For most of us, when we're hurting, checking our values compass is not the instinctual thing to do. Of course not! We've spent many years perfecting our craft of dealing with pesky monsters. We've become avoidance ninjas. But just like that skill, checking your values compass is another skill that takes a bit of practice to get in the habit of doing.

Remember the bear and apple story? This speaks both to our natural human instinct to move quickly away from pain and unpleasantness and our tendency to conflate external events (encounters with bears and apples) with internal events (our TEAMS). Using language, we learn to respond to scary internal events as if they were a big bear that could do us actual harm, and of course we respond accordingly (*This anxiety is too much; I can't stand this feeling of loneliness; I shouldn't be like this; there's something wrong with me*).

We all do away moves; there's nothing inherently wrong with them. It's just part of being human. Learning to avoid dangerous or threatening things has been a part of our survival routine for hundreds of thousands of years. It's through our away moves that we learn and grow. Away moves help illuminate our actions by providing a point of contrast. They give us information about who we are and what matters. So, we are definitely not saying don't do away moves (even though our monsters would *love* to use this as a rule to beat us around the head with).

For example, if you grew up with parents who were critical and judgmental, you may have developed a self-story about yourself as sometimes "not good enough." Understandably, you may have developed a number of strategies to make sure other people don't see this side of you. You're diligent at work, you're cautious and considerate in relationships, and you keep your opinions to yourself. And these may be excellent strategies to both protect yourself and actually endear yourself to others; you're probably a person other people quite like! But if you hold on too tightly to these strategies all the time, it may interfere with your choosing, for example, to be spontaneous, become intimate with others, or step out of your comfort zone.

The matrix helps us to remember that all the difficult TEAMS (again, thoughts, emotions, associations, memories, sensations) that show up—hurt, anger, pain, shame, all the different parts of our monsters—are not in fact the problem. It reminds us that the problem is how we respond to these experiences by trying to avoid or get rid of them. These TEAMS are the natural part of being human, especially for those of us who have had less than perfect upbringings. Time for a radical proposition: these TEAMS often speak to the very precious parts of ourselves, and we have to—and can—accept them in order to live lives of meaning that we value. With that, here are our last two questions:

In order to *never* experience your pain and suffering, what would you have to give up on and not care about?

____

____

____

____

If your pain and suffering in life were connected to those things that matter to you, would you choose to make room for the pain in order to have those things that are important to you?

____

____

____

WORKING WITH THE MATRIX

We'd like to suggest that you practice using the matrix over the week in relation to any situations where your self-esteem story gets triggered and your monster comes charging out, telling you you're a failure, you're inadequate, or whatever version is current. Complete the matrix form (available at http://www.newharbinger.com/43041) by thinking about what mattered to you, what monster appeared on the scene (and what TEAMS it comprised), what your autopilot responses were or could have been, and finally, if you were acting as the person you'd choose to be, what actions you would have taken.

As you fill out the week's matrix forms, observe whether it becomes easier to notice your monster at work. You may find that as you become more skilled at noticing it, it becomes easier to step out of autopilot responding. You might in fact find that by doing this, your values have a little more breathing space to become more prominent in your life. Make a note of any patterns you see emerging, using the following questions:

What patterns do you notice emerging? What have they shown about what's important to you and your relationship to your self-esteem story and monster? What do they show about your automatic responses? What have you learned about actions that reflect the kind of person you would like to be? What are the situations where your self-esteem monster tends to get louder and more insistent? What makes it easier to choose how to respond? What makes it harder? What skills does it highlight that you'd like to develop and strengthen?

____

____

____

____

____

____

IN SUMMARY

The matrix is a tool that gives us the chance to have a unique perspective on ourselves: our personal self-esteem monsters; our relationship with our thoughts, emotions, associations, memories, and sensations (TEAMS); and our own behavior and whether it's in the service on moving away from or toward what's important to us in life. But getting this perspective is less like a lightning bolt of insight and more an effortful skill that requires practice and development.

Now that you've seen how the matrix works, we're going to begin to make some actual changes. But first, we need to clear the decks and then build a solid foundation from which to launch off. It's likely that you've been living according to your self-story for some time now in autopilot mode, so we'd like to suggest an easier starting point to changing your self-care habits. This foundation will put you in good stead for the later bigger changes we'll be inviting you to make. So, on that note, let's move on to part 2 and talk about sleeping, eating, moving, and starting to do things you care about.

Bringing It All Together

Take a brief pause to consider what you have taken from this chapter. What have you learned about toward and away moves? As you reflect on this, what stands out to you in terms of key drivers for your actions?

____

____

As you consider the matrix, what patterns have you seen emerging that will be useful to be aware of?

____

____

Which quadrant in the matrix feels the most familiar and easiest to complete? Which one feels more difficult to complete? Why?

____

____

PART 2

The Self-Care Starting Point

CHAPTER 5

A Few Things That Help Us All: Some Basic Self-Care Principles

You can think of this chapter in terms of laying the foundation for those that follow it. Difficult self-stories can get in the way of our looking after ourselves in the most basic ways. This chapter is about reminding you of some of these basic self-care principles. As you go through it, it might be helpful to notice what your mind says to you about the various ideas presented here. If you notice thoughts like *I don't deserve to take better care of myself* or *My needs aren't important,* you could think about using the matrix to look at those thoughts in the context of pursuing a value of self-care. The matrix will also help you consider what choices you have in responding to those thoughts.

Most of us have access to a seemingly never-ending supply of self-help advice concerning everything from what to eat to how to spend our time. Hopefully, you will recognize that the last thing we want to do here is give you a bunch of extra rules to follow. One thing that is striking about the various people who come to us for help is that they tend to have no shortage of knowledge and ideas about the areas of life in which they get stuck. Rarely is seeing a therapist anyone's first port of call—most people will have tried something else first, whether it is asking a friend for advice, searching the internet, or buying a self-help book. All of that advice adds to what we gained from our upbringing and the wise (or not so wise) counsel of other people we have encountered through the years. As a consequence, most of us will have lots of rules and guiding principles shaping our behavior. We should be crystal clear here: there is nothing intrinsically wrong with having rules, and...slavishly following those rules, come what may, can be really problematic. Most of our clients get themselves stuck *because* they always follow their rules and don't respond to them flexibly. This is often because of a self-story that says, "These are the rules and they must be followed. If you don't follow them, then bad things will happen." Thus, we don't want to give you "must have" advice or rigid prescriptions for self-care, as we don't think that would be helpful. Think of what follows as a self-care buffet. We are inviting you to step up and take a look at some of the available dishes. You don't have to eat any of them, yet you might feel more nourished if you do. See if you can approach the buffet with curiosity and just notice what happens. What dishes would you choose if you could genuinely approach the buffet with a spirit of kindness and self-acceptance? In addition to thinking about *what* dishes you might choose, try and turn your attention toward *why* those choices are important in the context of building the life that you want. The point is that even a mundane trip to the grocery store can be transformed into something much more meaningful if you recognize that you are doing it because the meal you will ultimately cook represents a really nurturing decision on your part.

Try to approach this chapter with some flexibility, considering each suggestion in terms of how it might best relate to you and how you would like to live your life.

WHAT DO HUMAN BEINGS NEED?

Here's an interesting, if somewhat downbeat, fact about human beings. We are the only species on the planet that is known to die by suicide. No other animal is known to do it, not even lemmings, contrary to the popular urban myth. If a lemming falls into the water during the chaos of a mass migration, it will fight to try and save itself, whereas it is not unknown for a human who has jumped from a bridge in a suicide attempt to get out of the water and try again if the first attempt was unsuccessful. Suicide has been observed throughout history and across cultures and is sadly a very widespread behavior among humans, while being absent elsewhere in nature. Why would this be? What do only *we* have that gives rise to such a destructive urge, which appears to go so against our instincts for survival? What is it that makes us suffer so greatly? We are not claiming to have all the answers here, although it seems reasonable to wonder if it might have something to do with the darker side of language that we spoke about in chapter 1. Those clever minds of ours are able to imagine and experience concepts like hopelessness, worthlessness, and shame, which would be very hard to do without a language to do it with. Once we can appreciate how horrible it can be to feel those things, we can start to understand how tempting it might be to want to escape from them forever.

One of the gifts/curses of language is that it always operates in two directions. Let's focus on the gift part of this just now. If we can imagine someone being so hopeless as to want to end their life, we can also imagine someone having a life so rich and meaningful that they want to live it to the fullest. Of course, the $64,000 question here is, "What is it that makes life rich and meaningful?"

Unfortunately, we don't have a precise, one-size-fits-all, $64,000 answer, since it is very different for different people. Instead, we are going to focus on some areas of life that research has suggested are fundamental in sustaining human vitality and well-being.

As with everything in these kinds of conversations, opinions will differ on the question of what human beings need to be healthy and what things drive people toward self-destruction when they are absent from their lives. We have drawn our inspiration for the domains that fuel better self-care from two main sources: first, psychologist Kelly Wilson (2013), and second, the "five-a-day for mental health" campaign promoted by the National Health Service (2016) in the United Kingdom. We hope that what follows will serve as a useful pointer for building on existing strengths or starting to make some helpful changes.

Stay Clear of Things That Are Bad for You

It is very common for people to tell you that avoidance is bad. You might even read a version of that idea somewhere in this book. However, we hope that if you read it here, we have been careful enough to put some context around it. The thing is, for any organism to thrive, it needs to learn a variety of strategies for dealing with the things it comes into contact with. This includes avoidance. The previous chapter introduced us to the notion of toward moves (moving toward things that we want) and away moves (moving away from what you don't want). Both of these are equally important for a healthy life characterized by a good repertoire of self-care behaviors. Put another way, learning to say no is just as important as learning to say yes.

Human beings are quite fragile, and there are some things that are just bad for all of us, such as extremes of temperature, toxic chemicals, or jumping out of a plane without a parachute. However, each of us could probably compile a list of things we should steer clear of that might be a little more subtle and individualized. We invite you to give it some thought. Are there certain foods you know it's better not to eat? Certain situations that bring out the worst in you? Certain people you know you don't do well around? In the service of building up a repertoire of self-care behaviors, we invite you to identify up to five potential "banana skins" that you might be better off sidestepping.

In the interests of taking better care of myself, I would be better off if I kept away from:

____

____

____

____

Now, having identified these things, think carefully about how rigidly you want to apply your avoidance. These things might be best avoided all of the time or only in certain situations. For example, you might know that you can drink alcohol quite happily at a family meal, although if you drink on your own late into the night when you feel down, it never ends well. Try to think flexibly where you can. The aim is making wiser choices moment to moment. Remember, what works well for you one day or in one particular context might not work so well the next day or if the context changes.

Eat Real Food

This feels like one of those areas where it would be very easy to slip into a mode of preaching to you and telling you to follow some diet or other. We are going to try and avoid doing that, save for just reflecting on the fact that human beings did not survive for thousands of years eating the diet that has become commonplace in so-called developed nations. The widespread consumption of processed food and a diet rich in sugar has certainly not helped our health and well-being.

Rather than recommend some prescribed diet plan that may or may not suit your particular constitution, we are going to presume that you already have a reasonable idea of what kind of dietary intake helps you feel fit and healthy. One way of tuning in to this is to use the principles of the matrix described in the previous chapter. You might ask yourself what your diet looks like when you're feeling good and living in accordance with your values. You might also ask yourself what it looks like when you are stressed, and what you eat and drink when you are trying to chase away the blues. We are going to bet that the comparison is quite stark and that one set of food choices looks quite different from the other. If you based the major part of your diet on toward moves, this is probably going to be better for your self-care, although it is obviously important to retain some flexibility, since rigidly pursuing a puritanical approach to eating super-healthily rarely works out long term. Everyone benefits from a treat once in a while. For any readers interested in a more detailed look at managing your diet from a similar perspective to that which we have taken in this book, we would recommend *The Weight Escape* (Ciarrochi, Bailey, and Harris 2015).

Move Your Body

Several decades ago, if you told someone that you were going for a run, people would probably ask you, "Where to?" or "Who from?" Running generally wasn't something people did for its own sake as they were naturally more active and may not have needed to find the time to exercise. In the developed world we have become increasingly sedentary as technology and working patterns have reshaped our lives, and slowly and surely, the act of running has become a bona fide activity in its own right. Given the compelling research evidence, it seems obvious that we should all try to incorporate regular exercise into our schedules. Of all the things listed in this chapter that serve a value of self-care, it is probably the most essential to attend to. Research findings (National Health Service 2018) suggest that people who engage in regular physical activity have:

- up to a 35% lower risk of coronary heart disease and stroke
- up to a 50% lower risk of type 2 diabetes
- up to a 50% lower risk of colon cancer
- up to a 20% lower risk of breast cancer
- a 30% lower risk of early death
- up to an 83% lower risk of osteoarthritis
- up to a 68% lower risk of hip fracture
- a 30% lower risk of falls (among older adults)
- up to a 30% lower risk of depression
- up to a 30% lower risk of dementia

When you read the above list, regular exercise, defined as at least 150 minutes of physical activity over a week, starts to look like a miracle cure. Best of all, it doesn't have to cost anything and you can do it almost anywhere. Unfortunately, there is an antidote that can cancel out the benefits of the miracle—sitting or lying down. It turns out that even if you hit your target of 150 minutes of physical activity, the benefits of this are lost if you spend the rest of your time being inactive (so, go easy on those mindfulness exercises!).

As with the other areas of life listed in this chapter, we are not seeking to tell you what to do... however, in the service of improving your health and well-being, it might be helpful to review your activity levels. The quick exercise below can help you to do this—you can do it standing up if you like...

If you could work toward doing 150 minutes of reasonably vigorous physical activity each week, what might this comprise? List three activities that you could do regularly. They might be adaptations to existing activity (e.g., cycling to work instead of driving). If you are already hitting your target, you could list how you are currently achieving this as a reminder of some of the ways you already invest in your self-care.

____

____

____

If you could reduce the amount of time you spend being inactive, what adaptations might you make to your existing routine? List three changes you could make without too much difficulty (e.g., standing when you speak to your friend on the phone rather than sitting).

___

___

___

Get Enough Sleep

In tandem with a gradual decline in physical activity over recent decades, people in modern society are also getting a whole lot less sleep. Evidence suggests that around seven to nine hours of sleep each night is the optimum amount for most adults, and that regularly getting significantly more or less than that is associated with various health problems and even early mortality. Far from the popular philosophy of "work hard, play hard—I'll sleep when I'm dead," it is now pretty clear that the opposite is true and that the right amount of good quality sleep is one of the things that makes you thrive. With regard to self-care, the benefits of looking after your sleep are wide-ranging, including rebuilding muscles, processing emotions, and regulating your immune system, appetite control, metabolic function, and ability to maintain a healthy body weight. Going to sleep and getting up at roughly the same time each day also helps maintain your internal clock.

There are different approaches to managing your sleep, although many rely on having lots of rules and attempting to control the various factors that influence sleep. The problem with these approaches is that none of them are used by people who naturally sleep well. As our colleague Guy Meadows, sleep physiologist, wisely said, "No one ever struggled themselves to sleep." If you are wanting to attend to this area of your life, we would recommend thinking about what you already know works for you in terms of maintaining a healthy routine. There are some sensible precautions to think about, such as not drinking alcohol or caffeine too close to bedtime, although it is probably not that helpful to develop lots of rules about your bedtime routine since these can become a source of stress and anxiety. One simple guideline is to keep bedtime boring and not surround yourself with things that are stimulating and therefore likely to wake you up, such as televisions, phones, or other electronic devices. Think about how to make your bedroom comfortable, cool (63–66 degrees Fahrenheit or 17–19 degrees Celsius), dark, and quiet.

The other thing worth thinking about is how you manage those inevitable periods when you find it difficult to sleep. It probably won't surprise you to learn that stressing about being awake isn't going to help you sleep. So work toward mindful acceptance of being awake, rather than fighting to get yourself to sleep. Sleep is one of those paradoxical human functions where the more you try to control it, the further away it gets from your grasp. Mindfully accepting insomnia when it occurs has the benefit of allowing you to stay in bed and conserve your energy, as opposed to frustratedly walking around the house in a search for something (e.g., a book, a drink, the TV) that will help you get to sleep.

If you are interested in learning more about applying the principles that we use in this book to the area of sleep, we recommend that you visit https://www.thesleepschool.org and read *The Sleep Book* (Meadows, 2014).

Connect with Other People

As discussed in chapter 1, human beings are inherently social creatures who have evolved in social groups for thousands of years. It is therefore no surprise that for the vast majority of us, meaningful connections with other people are very important for our sense of emotional well-being. From the opposite perspective, one of the ultimate sanctions used against prisoners in correctional institutions is being held in solitary confinement, away from other people. This punishment is used precisely because it is so aversive. When we facilitate work on uncovering what it is that *really* matters with our clients or in trainings that we run, the vast majority of the time it is meaningfully connecting with others that comes at or near the top of the list. It is not the same for everyone, so there is no need to feel bad if this doesn't apply to you. However, if it does, we would invite you to think about whom it might feel important to connect with and what the best ways of doing that might be.

Modern life and changes in technology are transforming the ways in which we connect with each other. It is easy to rush to judgment about social media connections being no substitute for face-to-face connections. Maybe that's true; maybe it isn't. It's a relatively new phenomenon, and perhaps time and future research will tell us more. For now, what seems important is to figure out what types of connection work for you and invest in your self-care by pursuing them.

List three people, or groups of people, whom connecting with would be a genuine self-care move for you. (Feel free to pick fewer or more than three if it makes sense to.)

____

____

____

Next, list three things you could do to maximize your connection with those people. Try and be specific in terms of actions you could do, or do more of.

____

____

____

Engage in Meaningful Activity

This entry in our list might overlap with the previous one, since many of the activities that mean the most to us are shared with others. If that's the case for the things you enjoy doing, that's great. It's also important for some of us to engage in activities that are more about spending time with ourselves. What are the activities that light you up? What gives you a sense of meaning and purpose? It can be important to have things in our lives that meet the human desire for achievement, challenge, and personal growth. As stated in chapter 4, it probably matters less *what* it is that you spend your precious time doing because the more important part of it is the *why*.

Chapter 11 will deal with how to work out what really matters in more detail. For now, just pause and think about the activities you do, or could do, that would mean the most to you in terms of the kind of person you would like to be. What are they? What is the *why* that sits behind the *what?*

Keep on Learning

It can be easy to think of learning as something that finished when you left school. We prefer to think of learning as a lifelong adventure, and we would argue that engaging in ongoing opportunities to learn new things is good for our well-being. Ongoing learning is associated with greater satisfaction and an improved ability to manage stress. It can also help build confidence, help strengthen our sense of purpose, and help us connect with other people.

If you have negative associations with your time in school, rest assured that continuing learning does not need to mean taking more qualifications or sitting for more exams. We would encourage you to take a broad view of what it could be. It could involve anything from gaining more knowledge through reading a book to acquiring a new skill or talent via joining a group. It might even be as simple as continuing to pursue an interest that you're already quite familiar with.

Like many of the areas covered in this list, having the intention to learn is a great start. Committing to actually doing it is where we often fall short. Not very far from the laptop on which this book is being written is a bookshelf with lots of very shiny books on it. It doesn't take a genius to figure out why they look so brand new. Buying them was the easy part. Committing to reading them always seems to be a bit more of a challenge.

If learning is something that feels meaningful to you, use the space below to identify one activity that you could either start or do more of that would further your learning. You could also list some specific actions you would need to do that would make your learning possible, as well as some things that might get in the way and how you will handle them if they do (e.g., *I want to read one of those books on the shelf. To do that I'll need to block out some time, so I'm going to go to bed a half hour earlier each night and read then. I'll probably get distracted by the TV and want to stay up too late. If that happens, I'll try and notice that I'm getting sucked in and remind myself of the value of learning and why reading is important to me*).

____

____

____

____

____

Give to Others

If you have been born and raised in a developed nation at pretty much any time within the last century, you will have been surrounded by messages suggesting that the accumulation of stuff, whether in the form of money or possessions, is undeniably a good thing. Having "more" is generally prized within many of the cultures in which we live, so much so that not having "enough" of something, whether it is money, status, friends, "likes" on social media, or whatever, is a frequent source of our distress and discontent. However, since the twentieth century marked a transition point in which, for the first time in human history, more people died from issues related to having too much (e.g., obesity, diabetes) rather than not enough (e.g., starvation, lack of resources), it is worth questioning how good the relentless pursuit of "more" is for us.

It also seems worthwhile to question whether, in addition to accumulating and consuming, giving might actually be good for us too. There is evidence to suggest that acts associated with giving, whether donating unwanted items to charity, volunteering one's time, or helping support others, is good for our well-being and therefore serves a value of self-care. As with previous areas outlined in this chapter, we would encourage you to adopt a broad definition of giving, and if you are wanting to take steps in this direction, perhaps you could start by thinking of the smallest meaningful steps you might take, such as expressing gratitude to someone else, helping out a friend or a colleague, or offering some time or a skill that you have to a local project. Larger steps might involve regular commitments of time, such as volunteering for a charity. Once again, there are likely to be crossovers with previous items in our self-care list since acts of giving often bring us in touch with meaningful activity as well as closer connections with others.

Be Mindful

Last but not least in our list of self-care areas is the ultimate crossover item, since being mindful is something that you can do alongside every one of the others. The very nature of our noisy and talkative minds, coupled with the fast paced, "always on" mentality of modern life, can make it very difficult to be present. We spend a lot of time lost in rumination over the past or worry about the future. Trying to bring a more mindful and present-focused awareness to our daily lives can be challenging. However, both Eastern philosophical traditions and modern science have lots to say about the benefits of being mindful. Since chapter 7 will deal with the idea of mindfully "tuning in" in much greater depth, at this point, we will just invite you to pause and take notice of your thoughts, feelings, and bodily sensations in this moment. What is showing up for you right now as you head toward the end of this chapter? In particular, what do you notice that is relevant to your self-story? Is there any judgment or self-criticism present? Is your mind going over past events or making any predictions about the future? Take a moment to notice whatever is present for you and think about what it might be telling you about what is important.

Self-Care: Your Unique Needs

Before concluding this chapter, we would like you to spend a moment considering whether the above list of self-care domains covers everything relevant to you. We most likely won't have covered something that *you* think is really important because it is an area of your life that makes a real difference to you. It could be a relationship, an activity, or anything else that matters to you. If you think there is another area that you need to attend to in the service of self-care, make a note of it here.

____

____

____

____

IN SUMMARY

Despite all of the benefits of living today as opposed to at many previous points in human history, the pace of modern life makes it increasingly difficult to meet the basic requirements for a healthy life. It is much easier to imagine an individual in a hunter-gatherer society regularly addressing the items listed above than it is for many of us today. However, it is useful to remind ourselves that disconnection from these things is not good for us, and hopefully this chapter has served as a reminder of some important areas to attend to. We don't believe there is a single prescription for a healthy life, and we certainly don't want to tell you how best to look after yourself. However, we hope that the ideas and exercises in this chapter have helped you tune in to some choices you can make to build up your repertoire of self-care behaviors.

Given the close connection between the things that matter and our capacity for suffering (e.g., we tend to feel hurt about the same things in our lives that we really care about), it is entirely possible that reading through this chapter has given rise to some difficult thoughts and feelings about your sense of self. If this has happened, later chapters in the book will offer some more ideas about what to do when these experiences arise.

Bringing It All Together

Take a brief pause to consider what you have taken from this chapter. Of the different areas of life described as important to self-care, which ones do you feel motivated to prioritize? How might things be better if you did?

____

____

Next, complete the matrix that follows to identify what is important in relation to your value of self-care and how aspects of your self-story might interfere.

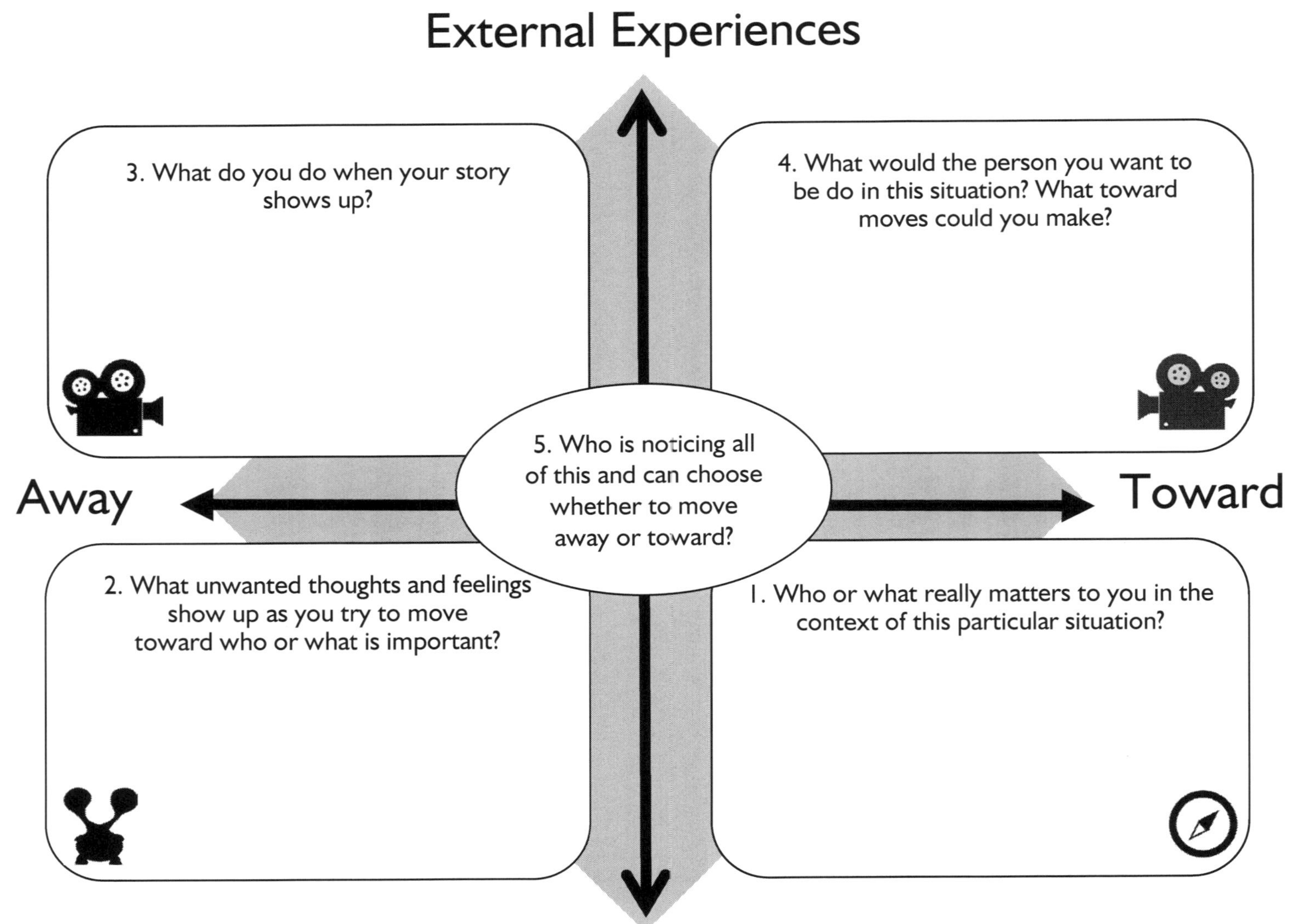
External Experiences
3. What do you do when your story shows up?
4. What would the person you want to be do in this situation? What toward moves could you make?
Away
5. Who is noticing all of this and can choose whether to move away or toward?
Toward
2. What unwanted thoughts and feelings show up as you try to move toward who or what is important?
1. Who or what really matters to you in the context of this particular situation?
Internal Experiences

CHAPTER 6

Introducing Self-Compassion

Now that we've been through some of the self-care habits that can help us take proper care of our bodies and live healthier lives, let's dive a little deeper into taking care of our minds. In this chapter, we'll explore the key to approaching our self-stories with acceptance: self-compassion. This practice opens the door to living in ways that really matter, which, as you've seen, our self-esteem holds us back from doing.

WHAT IS COMPASSION, ANYWAY?

The word "compassion" is derived from the Latin *compati*, which means "with suffering." The origins of the word point to the notion of suffering with or alongside someone or oneself. Compassion can motivate us to help alleviate suffering, but often it is as much about just being with someone when they are hurting. As a kind person once said to another person in pain, "If I can't help you see the light, I'll sit with you in the dark."

At its heart, being self-compassionate means becoming aware of our pain and our flaws and acknowledging them, rather than pretending they're not there or trying to fantasize them away. It means recognizing that having flaws, making mistakes, and being in pain is a human experience and therefore connects us with others, rather than isolating us. Finally, it means responding toward ourselves with acts of kindness, warmth, and acceptance—even, or especially, when our self-esteem monster is at its loudest.

Often, our flaws, the parts of ourselves we're insecure about or dislike, keep us from being able to view ourselves compassionately. The Japanese art form known as *kintsugi* provides us with insight into what you can do about this—and how self-compassion changes *how you feel about yourself.*

Kintsugi and the Art of Self-Acceptance

The Japanese art form of *kintsugi* involves repairing broken pottery in a unique way. Instead of working to *hide* the cracks, artists use gold to make the repair, thereby *emphasizing* the cracks. Kintsugi teaches something interesting about the scars of life we all bear but might instinctively hide away out of shame.

The artform is underpinned by a philosophy, *wabi-sabi,* that emphasizes understated beauty and taking pleasure in imperfection. Rather than relentlessly seeking to improve, wabi-sabi looks to celebrate things as they are, not as they should be. With regard to our self-stories, this suggests several notions that run counter to our typical flaw-focused self-stories. It says we can see value in our imperfections, as they make us unique and precious, and that we can work to embrace them. Crucially, it allows for permission to be yourself.

Like kintsugi, what are some of your own "imperfections" that give you character, uniqueness, and beauty?

____

____

Another way self-compassion is helpful is in terms of *what we want to achieve*—what we want to do with our lives, what we want our lives to be about. Remember, in quadrant 1 of the matrix is a question referring to your values: "Who or what really matters to you in the context of this particular situation?" If we were to extend this, we would want to ask, how are *you* included in this? If you were acting toward yourself in a way that was consistent with your values, how would that look? This is a particularly important question for those times in life when things are difficult or we are in pain. These will be the times when we are not at our best, and our relationship with ourselves is perhaps not at its best either. We might berate ourselves or tell ourselves that we should be feeling better and should stop whining or complaining. Sound familiar?

That's where self-compassion comes in. The demands of the modern age mean that we spend a lot of time moving between what psychologist Paul Gilbert calls our drive and threat systems (Gilbert 2005). The *drive system* is characterized by drive, motivation, and goal pursuit. The *threat system* focuses on threat detection and protection from anxiety often experienced in this mode. Gilbert also proposed a third system, called the *soothing system.* This system promotes care, compassion, and safety in the face of distress. It's this third system that tends to be hugely underutilized, particularly with people whose early environment didn't nurture or promote this system. Underutilizing your soothing system is a little like not using third gear in a car. If you're always in first or second gear, you run the risk of burning out your gearbox. Moving into third gear takes the pressure off, allows restoration, and makes for a much smoother ride.

Coach A or Coach B?

Take a moment to consider the following scenario:

Imagine you were about to learn a new skill. You've never done it before, and it's quite complicated and demanding, so you decide to enlist the assistance of a coach. You hear about two coaches who could help. They both come highly recommended, and you will get results whomever you pick.

Coach A is tough and harsh. She will drive you hard, never let you rest. Anytime you slack off, she will criticize you and pick up on any mistake you make. Even though she keeps you moving, it feels like she's sometimes being cruel.

Coach B is encouraging and kind. She helps you to set goals and will push you toward them, but she is supportive and motivating. When times get tough, she'll listen to you, but she'll also remind you of your skills and strengths in order to keep you motivated.

Remember, they both get the same results. So, which do you choose?

In our experience, most people choose Coach B. The idea of someone who is kind, supportive, and encouraging generally sounds much more appealing, especially if they get you the same results! However, outside the bounds of this hypothetical scenario, choosing Coach B is not always so straightforward because a number of common objections and worries surface. See if you recognize any from the list below. Put a check mark next to the ones that come up for you:

☐ If I'm kind to myself, then I won't drive myself and I won't achieve anything.

☐ I don't deserve to be kind toward myself.

☐ If I'm kind toward myself, I'll be letting myself off the hook.

☐ Being kind is a sign of weakness and I'd just be setting myself up for a world of pain.

☐ Being kind to myself is selfish or self-indulgent.

Any others you can think of? ____

____

Now, we don't want to discount these reasons automatically, because it's entirely possible they may be valid; that is, there's nothing wrong with being driven, keeping safe, and only being kind for deserving reasons. But we'd ask you first to listen to what sits underneath them. Think back to chapter 2, where we introduced the notion of your self-esteem monster. We'd like you to check out whether or not this is your monster showing up to sell you stories about yourself, like you're lazy, weak, or useless. If that's the case, then your reasons for not being kind to yourself may be based less on your own choices and more on the fact that you've been convinced that kindness is not for you because of who you are.

Based on the notion of moving toward self-acceptance that we introduced in chapter 3, here's an idea to consider: what if you're a complete and good-enough person just as you are? This doesn't mean that improvements can't be made or improvements aren't on the table. It's just that the basic starting point for whatever comes next is very different.

There is a pragmatic point to be considered, too. If rules like "Being kind to myself is self-indulgent" or "If I'm kind to myself, I won't drive myself to achieve anything" are in place for you, then you might be depriving yourself of valuable resources that come from the soothing system. It might be that you're whirring away in first or second gear when there's a whole other gear to be using.

It's Okay to Be Critical

Imagine you have a glass of salty water in front of you that you want to drink. As it is, the water is too salty to drink. One solution is to spend time attempting to pick out the grains of salt. With the aid of a powerful magnifying glass and some pretty fine tweezers, it might just be possible. But of course, there's an alternative. The trick is to add more *fresh* water into the glass. The amount of salt in the water remains the same, but proportionally, it lessens. Suddenly, what was undrinkable becomes drinkable. It's a little bit like that with critical thoughts. Let us explain.

Here's an important message we want to make sure isn't lost in all this talk about kindness and compassion. *It's okay to be critical of yourself.* It's fine to be judgmental, harsh, and demeaning. It's even okay to hate yourself. We're not here to say you shouldn't do those things or be that way toward yourself. In fact, we'd even say keep doing those things if you find them helpful at times. We recognize that you're not weird, crazy, or strange for being critical. It's a totally normal and human thing to do, and often it's borne out of circumstances that made it utterly understandable, useful, and necessary. The environments some of us grew up in required us to push ourselves to keep high standards, keep ourselves safe by never showing weakness, or just desperately make sense of a chaotic or neglectful environment by telling ourselves we are the problem, not our parents. However, over time, as we practice self-compassion, we can fill ourselves with kinder thoughts. And while the critical thoughts don't go away—that, as we've discussed, is a misconception about self-esteem and about the nature of negative thoughts, which are inevitable—they *do* come to seem less important and to have less impact.

Sometimes, the problem is just that terms like "compassion" and "kindness" are hard to sit with. Perhaps because they don't sound tough or come across as weak. This is somewhat ironic because most often being kind and compassionate with ourselves and others requires deep reservoirs of strength. Of course, it's important to find words that work for you. If "self-compassion" or "kindness" don't feel like quite the right fit, here are some of our favorite alternatives:

- Acting with integrity toward yourself
- Treating yourself with warmth
- Trusting yourself
- Backing yourself
- Being honest with yourself
- Being your own best coach
- Cutting yourself some slack
- Accepting the difficult stuff

Which ones resonate for you? Is there another term you prefer?

____

____

SELF-COMPASSION STRATEGIES

In this next section, we're going to introduce you to several of our favorite self-compassion exercises, ones we use regularly in our therapy practice and in our personal lives. They are designed to be practical and simple, but feel free to adapt them to fit your needs. We'd also encourage you to enter into this practice in the spirit of experimentation. Be curious. Notice what the experience is actually like (rather than what your mind predicts it's going to be like). Give things a go.

Self-compassion is multifaceted and complex and requires guts, determination, and skill. Practicing it well requires the ability to be mindfully present and the ability to gain distance from negative thoughts, which allows you to de-fang/de-claw your self-esteem monster—skills you'll work to develop later in this book (so you may want to come back to this chapter once you've completed those chapters). But let's start with the "simple" stuff and get a look at what being kind to yourself looks like, boots on the ground.

IMAGINE THIS...

Part 1: The World's Best Therapist

We'd like you to imagine for a moment that you came across the world's best therapist. This therapist is able to adapt to be perfect for you, helping you get to where you want to in life. They work hard for you and are also kind and understanding at the same time. See if you can bring an image of this person to mind. Write below what they look like, what clothes they wear, and what kind of expression they have on their face.

____

____

What kinds of things does the therapist say...

To motivate you?

____

____

To soothe you when you hurt?

____

____

To challenge and push you?

____

____

When you've screwed up and made a mistake?

____

____

Okay, cards on the table. What we're asking you to do is start getting a compassionate language up and running. The attitude and stance of support, warmth, and kindness, especially in the face of adversity, is what we'd like to you consider carrying forward in terms of how you behave with yourself. In the next part, we want to bring it a little closer to home.

Part 2: Your Loved One

We'd like you to bring someone to mind whom you love and care about. Someone for whom you truly and genuinely want the best in life. Now, imagine you find them in a state of hurt, anguish, or suffering. And suppose there isn't anything immediate to be done to take away their hurt; for example, they've lost someone close to them, they've experienced a relationship breakup, or they've received some painful news. What would you say to them so that they understand you recognize their pain? What kind words would you offer them? How could you acknowledge their hurt without attempting to push it away?

Write down the things you would say here:

____

____

____

____

Our proposal is that the essence of these words represents your intuitive ability to apply kindness and compassion. We would suggest that these are the kinds of words and gestures that you could apply to yourself in the times in life when you are hurting.

Take some time now and reflect on the last two parts of this exercise. What have you learned about the kinds of messages that you would like to give yourself? What kinds of things you would you like to keep in mind? Make some notes below:

____

____

____

____

Part 3: Your Advisor

For this final part of the exercise, pause for a few moments and imagine the face of someone you love and trust. Someone who would always want the best for you. This person might be a friend, a loved one, or someone you don't actually know, like a personal hero of yours. They will be like a trusted advisor who will be with you for the exercise, in spirit if not physically.

Now imagine a difficult situation you are dealing with or negative feelings you are having about yourself. And imagine that you are standing face to face with your trusted advisor. Now, try a harder thing. Imagine you are looking back at yourself through their eyes.

Consider each of these questions, pausing a while after each one.

- Want do you imagine that they are thinking in this moment?
- What do they want for you out of today?
- How would they want you to be?
- What qualities would they want you to embody?
- How would they want you to act?
- What difficult thoughts and feelings would they know you might have to make room for?
- What stand would they want you to take toward those more difficult things?

See if you can get in touch with the kindness and compassion you know that they would have for you in this moment. Now look back at your advisor through your own eyes. Notice what you feel toward them. If you could distill your response to them in to one sentence, what would you say?

____

____

Finally, consider how to honor what your advisor would want for you. If you wish, you could make a commitment to yourself that you will try to act in at least one of the ways you have just considered today. You might also want to commit to being kind to yourself if anything difficult arises that gets in the way of that commitment. Make some notes about what that commitment could involve:

____

____

How we hold our body can be very important for self-compassion. Although it's often exceedingly difficult to control how we feel, we can have far more control over how we act, how we move, and what we do with our body. Practicing self-compassion is not about feeling a certain way, but far more about acting in particular ways toward ourselves.

This next exercise is designed to be used in those moments when you are hurting or are in pain. It's not aimed at taking away the pain, but, with kindness and warmth, simply acknowledging that it is there. We'd like you to practice this first.

COMPASSIONATE SOOTHING

Get into a nice comfy position somewhere you can sit for five to ten minutes. Prop your book or device up on something so you can read hands-free, or download the audio recording of this exercise at http://www.newharbinger.com/43041.

1. First, turn your attention to your breath. We'd like you to regulate your breathing to slow it down and get big, full breaths that fill out your lungs right down to your diaphragm. On the in-breath, count "in, 2, 3, 4, 5," hold for a second, then breathe out, counting "out, 2, 3, 4, 5," counting about one second each. Do this for about a minute.
2. Next, bring to mind a time in the last few weeks when you remember feeling in pain, upset, or hurt. See if you can drop back into the memory, so much so that you can bring the feeling back into the present with you now.
3. Observe the feeling in your body, noticing where it's located. Notice the size of the feeling, its shape, and its boundaries.
4. Now, see if you can give the feeling a name. Use descriptive words (rather than judgmental evaluations) such as "sadness," "tension," "anger," or "heaviness."
5. Notice all the judgments and evaluations that come rushing forward in the presence of this feeling. See if you can simply allow these to be there and let go of the need to respond to these.
6. Now, soften into the feeling. Take your hand and place it on your body, over where you are feeling the emotion, a bit like you would to soothe someone close to you. Let this gesture represent warmth, understanding, and kindness. These aren't feelings you have to have, but rather this is an action.
7. As you're doing this, become aware of your breathing. As you breathe in, imagine you are breathing in space, in and around the emotion, so as to give it a bit more room to move. And as you breathe out, bring warmth to the feeling.

Here's another exercise to help promote self-compassion.

COMPASSIONATE UNDERSTANDING EXERCISE

In this exercise, designed to be used at times in life when you are especially hurting, we'd like you to spend some time writing a letter to yourself in which you practice expressing warmth and kindness. As you're writing, hold in mind the kind of tone you would like to express toward someone you cared about at a point when they were hurting. We'd also like you practice being understanding toward yourself—able, for instance, to forgive yourself for mistakes you might have made. Use the following prompts for the letter:

What is the situation that led to my feeling hurt or upset?

____

____

____

What am I feeling right now? Where in my body am I holding my emotions?

____

____

What is my self-esteem monster saying right now? About me? About feeling as I do? How is it criticizing me?

____

____

In what ways does my monster help? How does it make me feel better? How does it make me feel safer? How does it help me feel normal or in control?

____

____

What kind, compassionate things could I say to myself right now? How could I show myself understanding? What words could I use to demonstrate warmth toward myself?

____

____

In what ways does being compassionate toward myself scare or worry me? What would I have to let go of or give up to be kind?

____

____

What important life direction or value is at play here? If I were in charge, rather than my self-esteem monster, what actions would I choose to take? With my feelings? In regard to the situation?

____

____

Do you remember Ruby from chapter 2? She's gone through a difficult experience that brought up lots of painful emotions, and she completed the letter writing exercise. Let's see what she said.

What is the situation that led to my feeling hurt or upset?

I was so nervous at Tasha's big birthday dinner with all her glamorous friends I didn't know and I drank way too much. I made an idiot of myself. Everyone could see I was drunk.

What am I feeling right now? Where in my body am I holding my emotions?

I feel acute embarrassment and shame. I also feel anxious about having to talk to anyone from last night. It's like a ball in the pit of my stomach.

What is my self-esteem monster saying right now? About me? About feeling as I do? How is it criticizing me?

You're a fucking idiot. Why do you always do this? Everything you touch turns to shit and you screw up everything.

In what ways does my monster help? How does it make me feel better? How does it make me feel safer? How does it help me feel normal or in control?

It feels good to hear that, because it helps me keep myself in check. It also means no one else can hurt me by saying this. I know they're thinking it, but this is a preemptive strike.

What kind, compassionate things could I say to myself right now? How could I show myself understanding? What words could I use to demonstrate warmth toward myself?

It's OK, it's not the worst thing in the world to do. You weren't out to harm anyone, you just got carried away. It's OK to make mistakes. Other people also make mistakes, you're not the only one.

In what ways does being compassionate toward myself scare or worry me? What would I have to let go of or give up to be kind?

It scares me to be kind to myself. I worry about letting myself off the hook and doing the same thing again, like I always do. It also means I may actually have to take proper responsibility and make amends. Beating myself up is normally enough.

What important life direction or value is at play here? If I were in charge, rather than my self-esteem monster, what actions would I choose to take? With my feelings? In regard to the situation?

I'm important. I want to take actions that are helpful to me. I get why I beat myself up, but it's never worked before. Plus, it's just all old stuff from the past my dad used to say to me. I want to be kind and understanding toward myself. I also want to apologize to Tasha and explain to her why I was so nervous.

We've put these prompts into a handy worksheet format for you to practice on. If you find it helpful, you can download additional copies of this worksheet at http://www.newharbinger.com/43041.

Compassionate Prompt Sheet

Describe the situation.	Describe how are you feeling.	What is your self-esteem monster saying to you?	How is your monster helping?	What kind things could you say to yourself?	What do you need to let go of to be kind?	What value is at play here? What actions would you choose to take?

PRACTICING SELF-COMPASSION IN TOUGH SITUATIONS

Of course, it's easy to use these strategies to accept yourself when everything is plain sailing. The real trick is being able to practice acceptance, kindness, and compassion when things are not going so well. Now that you've had some opportunities to practice self-compassion, we'd like to help you think about how to translate these into actual life, where you can practice these strategies at those particularly difficult points. It's these difficult points where it can be easy to respond in autopilot mode, and we can end up in a downward spiral with our self-esteem monster. Here are some situations in which we'd like you to move up to your third gear using self-compassion. Practice while:

- Getting rejected—if you meet enough people, some will reject you
- Performing poorly at something
- Being negatively evaluated
- Putting yourself first
- Being honest with others
- Disagreeing with people
- In the company of people you don't like
- Doing something embarrassing

IN SUMMARY

Again, self-compassion works like a third gear and as an alternative to the drive and threat system gears. It provides an antidote to the powerful self-critical thoughts that self-esteem monsters love to throw at us. It seeks to provide comfort, safety, and soothing when we're hurting. It allows us to connect better with ourselves and others when we are in pain.

Most of us find it far easier to be kind and understanding toward other people than to ourselves. We hold on to powerful rules that get in the way of applying kindness and compassion to ourselves—rules that seek to drive us forward relentlessly but that are often based on outdated stories we hold about ourselves. Self-compassion doesn't mean letting ourselves off the hook; it doesn't mean we sink into a swamp of mediocrity or that we don't care about others. It does mean that YOU get to choose your relationship with yourself. Being self-compassionate, like any skill, takes practice.

Now that we have hopefully given you something to think about in terms of taking better care of yourself, part 3 will focus on six specific skills for developing self-acceptance. In the next chapter, we are going to focus on the first step to self-acceptance: the art and science of mindfully tuning in to your own body. This skill goes hand-in-hand with self-compassion.

Bringing It All Together

Take a moment to consider what this chapter has added to your understanding of compassion and self-compassion. What caught your attention as new or novel?

____

____

What does your self-esteem monster say about the prospect of kindness and compassion? What exercises feel like they are going to be useful? What feels like it is going to be challenging?

____

____

____

PART 3

Six Steps to Self-Acceptance

CHAPTER 7

Tuning In

Language is so dominant in our culture. Everything we do is so soaked in language that we swim in a virtual sea of it. We even have handy little devices to keep us in the language sea if we ever find ourselves on our own. With our computers and smartphones, we never need to be without language and communication of some form or another.

As much as this can be useful, it also means that we're plugged in to all the ways to compare, evaluate, and judge ourselves in relation to other people. Stepping out of this world has become increasingly difficult, if not impossible. And we would make the case that it's become increasingly important to manage this flow of language with awareness! So let's begin with the first step to self-awareness, tuning in to the present moment.

Do you ever find it difficult to just sit on your own? Doing nothing? Just your own thoughts to entertain you? Well, if you answered yes, you're in good company. It turns out most people find it exceedingly difficult to sit with their own thoughts, as confirmed in a study by psychologists from Harvard and Virginia Universities (Wilson et al. 2014). Researchers put people in a quiet, plain room, with no distractions except for a device that could administer decent electric shocks. Slightly weird, we hear you say, and you would not be wrong. But this is science! So hard was it for people to sit quietly with their own thoughts and do nothing that over a quarter of women and two thirds of men shocked themselves at least once during the fifteen minutes they were in the room. One poor chap administered 190 shocks to himself and was classified as an outlier, perhaps in more ways than one. All in all, a rather electrifying result wouldn't you say?

Why is it so difficult? Well, the results point to how driven we are to be busy *doing*.

ACTIVE VS. SENSING MODE

Here's an invitation. We'd like you to pause for a second and do something. This particular "something" is a little unusual. We'd like you to do *nothing*. Nothing at all for the next sixty seconds. Set a timer on your watch or phone, get comfy in your chair, take a deep breath, and then for the next minute, do nothing...

What was that experience like? If you are like most people, it's probable that while on the outside there wasn't much activity to see, on the inside your mind went crazy.

What am I doing?

What's the point of this?

Is time up yet?

I've got things to do!

I'm not relaxed. Am I even doing this right?

Hmm, there's my stomach rumbling. Must be lunch time soon. Right? Surely. Any minute now...

Sound familiar? Here's the thing. When we slow down what we're doing and create a little quiet, our minds often get very busy. If that happened to you, don't worry. You're like most other people. If you happened to have sixty seconds of blissful silence and quiet, then great. Savor that moment. But remember, your turn will come for the word machine to crank up again very soon!

What is actually happening here? Well, it's just your mind doing its thing. Minds love to be active. This *active mode* can include a range of activities:

- Problem solving
- Analyzing
- Worrying
- Planning
- Ruminating
- Mentally traveling through time
- Rationalizing
- Criticizing
- Focusing
- Catastrophizing

Some of these active skills are extraordinarily helpful. It's very useful to be able to plan and strategize. A bit of rumination that assists us in learning from mistakes can be productive. And some, of course, are naturally less helpful in that they get us more and more stuck.

There is another mode of mind, one that most of us have not developed or cultivated. Or if we have, we only apply it in a narrow part of our lives. This mode, sometimes called a *sensing mode,* includes qualities such as:

- Being in the moment without purpose or goals
- Having awareness of the five senses
- Being connected to the present moment
- Being observant of body states
- Being observant of emotions

This sensing mode of mind facilitates your coming back into the present moment. Which is an odd thing to say, because of course we're always in the present. But metaphorically, our minds "time machine" us all over the place. Consider the following questions:

- What did you have for breakfast this morning?
- What are you doing next weekend?
- What did it feel like when you last appreciated a beautiful sunset?
- When is your self-esteem monster likely to next give you a hard time?

Notice how easy it is to slip out of what's directly in front of you? There you are, sitting reading this book, in a plush, comfy armchair (or so we imagine), and suddenly, whoosh, you were transported to times and lands far away.

Just to note, there's nothing inherently wrong with this ability of ours. It's just that there are times when it can get us into trouble, for example:

- When we need to be focused in the moment, on what is in front of us
- When our thoughts pull us into judgment, evaluation, or criticism
- When our self-esteem traps us in unhelpful cycles of fearful worry or gloomy rumination
- When our monster blinkers our perspective, so we don't see the opportunities that are available to us

So, how do we do it then?

THE CASE FOR MINDFULNESS

There are a few things to keep in mind that point to the art and science of staying in the moment. First, the science. There has been a *ton* of research on the impact of developing the skill of mindfulness and staying in the present. Here are some highlights (Keng, Smoski, and Robins 2011; Khoury et al. 2013; Kimmes, Durtschi, and Fincham 2017). People who practice mindfulness:

- Are less stressed
- Have more fulfilling relationships
- Learn quicker and have better memory capabilities
- Have improved overall mental health and well-being
- Have better physical health
- Are happier and more content with life

We're sure you'll agree those results make quite a case for exploring this a little further.

Why are scientists getting these results from what seems to be such a simple activity? It turns out, as with most human-related things, this is a complicated question. It's likely to be because of a few factors, but principally, slowing down and pausing very deliberately reduces autopilot responding. This means we become more aware of our thoughts, emotions, and sensations, the circumstances within which they occur, and our behavior. Straightaway, we pop ourselves out of the behavioral stream and can see the flow of our experiences and links to our actions. This is a very powerful thing to be able to do, especially when it is *so* easy to respond to our self-stories in extremely automatic ways, which can often preclude taking action as we'd choose to.

The point is that when we step out of autopilot mode, we're more distanced from our experiences. They therefore become just that bit less threatening. We don't have to engage with them—we have the choice to allow them to flow by. This allows us to make choices and take actions that will promote well-being, health, and deeper connections with people in our relationships. From this place of equanimity, our own relationship with ourselves can be improved as kindness and acceptance toward our experience is fostered.

THREE STEPS TO MINDFULNESS

How then do we develop this skill? There are in fact many ways, and we're going to introduce you to a few of our personal favorites. But we'll start with the basics.

Although mindfulness is often spoken about as a Buddhist practice (which it is), practices that promote present moment-ness or mindfulness are common in both spiritual and secular communities. What we will present here is a secular psychological skill that can be practiced and developed. Just like building a muscle when you hit the gym, the ability to be mindful strengthens as you practice.

The practice has three essential steps:

1. Bring your attention into the present moment.
2. Get distracted as your mind wanders.
3. Bring your attention back to the present moment.

It is as simple as that. But just because it is simple doesn't mean it is straightforward. Let's break each of these steps down.

1. Bring your attention into the present moment.

   This requires you to make a deliberate choice about where your attention goes to. Your attention is a little like a spotlight that you have your hands on, but sometimes it has a mind of its own. When practicing, it's useful to have an anchor where you can let your attention rest. Anchors can include:

- Something you can feel, like the rhythm of your breath or the position or movement of your body
- Something you can hear inside or outside of you
- Something you can smell, like hot coffee or warm bread
- Something you can taste, like the delicious taste of Ben and Jerry's chocolate fudge brownie ice-cream
- Something you can see, such as the particular details of the font you are reading right now

The idea is to come to the present moment with a sense of curiosity in order to become aware of what actually is present in the moment, rather than what our minds say is there. In this way, we're dialing down the importance of our busy, problem-solving minds.

2. Get distracted as your mind wanders.

   We are not going to promise you many things in this book, but here's one: your mind is going to wander, and you will be distracted. It's how it goes. You might find your mind instantly goes bananas and floods you with thoughts. Or you might find that you experience a deep and tranquil calm. But eventually your mind will pipe up with something. Which moves us swiftly onto point three.

3. Bring your attention back to the present moment.

   When your mind wanders, your task is then to notice this and bring your attention back to the present, specifically to the anchor you have chosen, be it your breath, your body, or one of your five senses.

   Now keep in mind that you will fail spectacularly at this simple task. And by fail, we mean you will get lost in thought and become distracted. That will happen and you will fail. So, given that's out of the way, you now have nothing to achieve or succeed at. You have permission to approach this task with a spirit of openness, curiosity, and creativity.

LET'S PRACTICE

The following is a collection of our favorite exercises that we routinely use and teach people to help them develop their mindfulness skills. We hope that within this collection, you'll find something that works well for you and your lifestyle. To that end, we'd recommend trying out each of them several times to find the ones that work best for you. You can download the audio files of these exercises at http://www.newharbinger.com/43041.

CHECKING IN

We'd encourage you to practice this first in a particular way, just to get the hang of it. Once you're familiar with the exercise, you can do it anywhere, at any time: when you're driving to work, before you head out for a date, when you're exercising.

Find a comfy place to sit, and adjust your body into an upright and alert position. Imagine there is a piece of string going through your spine and out the top of your head that for a moment gently holds your posture up, and then release it so you can settle.

We're going to do several "check ins" of what's going on under your skin. The purpose here is to simply become aware and check in.

> *Bring your attention to your body and begin to check in with your body, noticing how you physically feel. Take thirty seconds to scan your body, from feet to head, to notice any sensations in your body. Notice aches, tensions, points of relaxation. Just become aware of each sensation without changing it. Just notice and allow it to be there.*
>
> *Now, move your attention to your breathing and check in with your breath. Become aware of all that is involved in the breathing process. The rise and fall of your chest. The expansion and contraction of your abdomen. The air moving in and out of your nose or mouth. Just become aware of each part of breathing without changing it. Just notice and allow it to be there.*
>
> *Now, move your attention to your mind. Check in with the overall quality of your mind. Notice whether your mind is busy or slow. Whether the quality of thoughts is kind, critical, curious, or judgmental. Just become aware of your mind at work, without changing it. Just notice and allow it to be there.*

MINDFUL BODY AND BREATH

Mindful breathing is one of our favorite ways to come back into the present. The breath is with is us all of time and provides an excellent anchor. The following exercise is a way to practice coming back to the present moment using the breath.

> *Find a comfy place to sit with your legs uncrossed and your hands resting in your lap. Sit in an upright position that has a posture of dignity to it. Either close your eyes or find a point in front of you to focus on. Remember, these aren't strict rules, so do what works best for you.*
>
> *As you settle into the exercise, bring your attention to your body. Notice the sensation of sitting in your chair. Notice where your body contacts the chair and also where it doesn't. Bring your attention to your feet and notice the sensations there. Zoom right in to your left big toe and observe all the sensations that are present in your big toe.*

Now, moving your attention out, like a spotlight beam, bring your attention to your breath. Simply allow your attention to gather around the whole of the breathing process, as best as you're able. Observe your abdomen rising and falling and your chest moving in and out.

It's likely that you'll notice your mind wander at various points, and that's perfectly normal. When you notice your mind has wandered, escort it gently back to noticing your breath.

Continue to observe your breathing in operation, noticing the rise and fall of each cycle. See if you can be curious about each breath, in each moment, and how it is unique. As best as you are able, allow breathing to do its thing, for now. Just sit back and watch it without controlling it.

Finally, zoom your attention in to the point at which the air moves in and out of your nose or mouth. See if you can notice the details of this experience. The difference in temperature. The noise of the air. The feel of the in-breath versus the out-breath. There is no special goal here or anything particular to achieve. Just simply observe what is in your attention, in this moment.

MINDFULNESS OF SOUND

In this exercise, we're going to ask you to engage your hearing. Of course, there are many ways to do this, but for this exercise, we'd like you to listen to a piece of music. We have a particular track for this exercise, which you can find at http://www.newharbinger.com/43041. Read through the instructions below to get familiar with them before you listen to the music.

Find a quiet place to sit where you won't be disturbed while you listen to the piece. Before you press play, take a few moments to come into the present moment by bringing your attention to your breath. Just notice the steady rise and fall of your breath; allowing breathing to occur without changing it.

Now, press play on the recording. As the piece starts, see if you can attend to the different sounds you can hear. Notice as each sound and instrument is added in.

As the track builds, see if you can move your attention between the different sounds, separating each out. Notice the melody and how it flows and changes. Notice the rhythm, both its regularities and also any changes.

You may become aware of emotions that arise as you're listening to the music. Some may be pleasant, and some may be unpleasant. Acknowledge them as they occur and bring your attention back to the sounds within the music.

Now, shift your attention out and listen to the music as a whole. As best as you're able, listen to the piece as if it were a single, complete sound.

MINDFUL MOVEMENTS

It's often said that the body is the metaphorical gateway into the present. Our body is always taking place now, which can be in stark contrast to our time-traveling mind. Long traditions of yoga and tai chi are built on this knowledge to provide the many benefits from these approaches. There are three mindful body movements we'd suggest practicing.

Shoulder roll. *Bring awareness to your shoulders and notice the position you find them in. Imagine holding a bucket of rocks in each hand to drop your shoulders somewhat. Having done that, bring your shoulders up now and roll them back. Allow your arms to stretch outward as you do this. Let your whole chest open up and expand outward. Coordinate this whole movement with a slow and deep breath in. Take about five seconds to roll your shoulders back and breathe in at the same time. Slowly breathe out over five seconds and allow your shoulders to fall back to a resting position, holding a posture of alertness and dignity following the movement.*

Sky reach. *Clasp your hands in front of you with your fingers interlocked. Gradually bring your arms above your head so that your interlocked hands face upward toward the sky. As you're doing this movement, bring your attention to the different muscles and how they move. Now, gently extend up and reach for the sky, finding the point where you can feel your muscles stretch. Hold this position for five seconds, bringing awareness to your muscles. Now, gradually release the stretch and slowly bring your arms back down to rest with your hands still clasped in front of you. Take a moment to appreciate the contrast between this resting place and the stretch.*

Walking with awareness. *When walking, bring attention to the body movements involved in the process. Slow down for a moment so you can observe all the movements involved. Notice the sensations of transferring weight through one foot, from heel to ball, to the other foot, heel to ball. Become aware of the engagement of muscles on each leg. Observe the gentle swing of each arm as it coordinates with the overall movement. Notice your capacity to step back from all of this and just let it happen; watching as an observer as this symphony of movement takes place.*

MINDFULNESS ON THE MOVE

We typically engage in many routine activities each day that we repeat over and over each day, such as:

- Brushing our teeth
- Showering or bathing
- Traveling to work or school
- Checking our phone for messages

- Checking our social media updates
- Eating meals
- Drinking coffee, tea, or water
- Washing dishes or stacking the dishwasher
- Watching television
- Exercising

And the list goes on with these routine activities that we hardly have to think about because they are so automatic to us. What a great place to practice stepping out of autopilot mode and coming into the moment. The extra advantage is that these activities happen every day and represent regular opportunities to come into the present—which is a great antidote to a mind that says, *You're too busy to practice mindfulness!*

Our invitation to you is to pick one activity from the list above (or a different routine activity you do) and do it mindfully. Which is to say, interrupt the habitual way you normally do it. Here are some ways that you can do that:

Become ultra-interested in the activity you are engaging in. Imagine you are an alien scientist who has been beamed down into a human body and your task is to study this activity. What do you notice?

Slow the activity down to half speed. Make each movement precise and coordinated, as if you were a performance artist with a rapt audience intently watching your every move. Bring flow and grace to your actions and allow your attention to become wrapped around the experience of your movements.

Notice qualities that weren't previously apparent. Bring all of your five senses to the activity. For example, when brushing your teeth, notice the quality of the feel of the bristles against your gums. When drinking a cup of tea or coffee, engage with the sound of the liquid as it swirls around your mouth. When washing the dishes, notice all the variety of sounds you can hear. When watching TV, tune in to the emotions you experience.

LET'S DEBRIEF

So much of our time is spent in autopilot mode that we forget to check in with our body and return to the present. We miss important opportunities both to listen to our experience and also to return to the present. We'd like you to hold in mind some questions as you complete each of the mindfulness exercises we presented. Consider using the Mindfulness Recording Worksheet, which you can download at http://www.newharbinger.com/43041, to keep track of your practice and the changes and benefits you experience. Below are the key questions we'd like you to answer:

1. What did you observe or notice during the exercise? What was new? What was different from your expectations?
2. How close or overwhelming did your self-story (or self-esteem monster) feel before the exercise? How close or overwhelming does it feel now?
3. What benefits have you noticed? Less entangled? Less overwhelmed? More choice over your actions?

Mindfulness Recording Worksheet

Date	Which mindfulness exercise did you complete?	What did you observe or notice during the exercise? What was new? What was different from your expectations?	How close or overwhelming did your self-story (or self-esteem monster) feel before the exercise? How close or overwhelming does it feel now?	What benefits have you noticed? Less entangled? Less overwhelmed? More choice over your actions?

TROUBLESHOOTING

In our experience, there are a few obstacles that repeatedly come up for people as they are practicing mindfulness. We'd like to go through each of them here.

I'm Too Busy and I Don't Have Time for This!

Not to diminish the fact that you may indeed be extraordinarily busy, but saying you're too busy to practice mindfulness is a bit like saying you're too dirty to have a shower. Mindfulness allows you the capacity to manage more effectively and respond in ways that you choose. As the famous saying goes, "I'm too busy to rush," meaning that when we're at our capacity and running ragged, those are exactly the times to pause, slow down, and notice what is going on in the moment.

I Don't Feel Relaxed/Better/Happy

It's important to keep in mind that mindfulness is building the capacity to respond to everything our self-esteem monster throws at us more effectively. In the short term, doing something radically different, such as mindfulness, is going to feel a little odd or uncomfortable. The long-term aim, however, is to strengthen the muscle that allows you to be as effective as possible as big feelings, painful self-stories, and old habits pull at you. As you practice the above exercises, you may not feel relaxed, better, or happy. Sometimes painful feelings get the volume turned up on them as you notice them. And sometimes your self-esteem monster gets louder when you don't do what it wants you to. This is actually a sign you're on the right track. Like after a good exercise session or gym workout, your body may feel sore as its capacity has been stretched and developed.

I'm Too Distractible

Practicing mindfulness is unlike anything you're likely to do in the rest of your life. Deliberately stopping and doing nothing for no purpose: what a strange thing to do! It's highly probable your mind will go wild and you'll become very distracted. If you become overly focused on trying to control your mind, you'll find the whole experience highly aversive. So, as we mentioned earlier, the trick is to expect to be distracted and allow that to happen. It's human and completely fine. With a quality of warmth and compassion, you're learning the skill of noticing the points when your mind is distracted and then choosing where your attention goes to next. And our hope is that it's not only your self-story that gets all of your attention.

To make it especially easy, we've created a simple mindfulness "cheat sheet" for you. This is designed to make mindfulness accessible and practical to any situation you find yourself in, especially those where your self-story likes to show up. If you do only one thing from this chapter, this would be the thing we'd like you to do. You can download the Mindfulness Cheat Sheet at http:www.newharbinger.com/43041. Print it out or take a photo on your phone and keep it with you to remind yourself what to do.

MINDFULNESS CHEAT SHEET

Pause. Take a moment to stop what you are doing. Step out of the stream of habit, repetition, and automaticity and become aware of the present moment.

Find an anchor. This could be your breath, your body, or what you see, hear, taste, touch, or smell. Wrap your attention around that anchor.

What do you notice? Describe as accurately and objectively as you can what you notice in the moment.

Bring mindful qualities. As you notice, see if you can let go of any struggle with what's in the moment. Allow whatever shows up to be as it is. Breathe into the experience and soften up around it.

What matters? Now ask yourself, if you were able to choose an action that was consistent with the kind of person you'd like to be (and not how your self-story says you are), what action would that be?

IN SUMMARY

Strengthening your muscle to arrive in the present moment has many benefits in terms of developing your resilience, well-being, and life satisfaction. It is also a key way to build a healthier relationship with your self-esteem monster. If your monster would rather you spent all your time anxiously worrying and doubting yourself or ruminating on your past failures, mindfulness allows to you to arrive in the present moment and be with whatever is there. It can be the gateway to building a sense of self based on self-compassion, acceptance, and kindness, which will allow you to more fully participate in the stuff of life, whether that be strengthening connections, pursuing fulfilling achievements, or increasing your sense of pleasure or fun.

In the next chapter, we are going to offer a new perspective on how we think about ourselves. We've talked a great deal about the part of you represented by the monster. We've also talked about the other part of you that experiences the monster. We want to introduce you to the second step to self-acceptance: the idea of holding and containing these different parts of yourself. It's from this perspective that you'll be able to build resilience and truly make choices about the kind of person you want to be!

Bringing It All Together

Take a mindful pause at this point in the book. If you notice the urge to zoom off to the next chapter, see if you can just observe that urge while acknowledging our invitation to stop here for a moment.

What has stood out to you as important in the chapter? What has been new learning? Is there any old learning that has been refreshed as a result of reading this?

____

____

If you were to make one small change in your life after reading this chapter to be more mindful a little more often, what would it be?

____

____

CHAPTER 8

Noticing Who Is Noticing

To recap so far, in part 1, we talked about our self-stories, our relationships with them, and how at times these can get us into trouble...well, if not trouble, then certainly not living life to our fullest capacity or in the ways that we ourselves would choose. But sometimes it feels like there just is no other way to even think about living life. Even the notion of a "self-esteem monster" can seem patently ridiculous. Because these aren't stories, you tell yourself, they're actually true! In part 2, we introduced the concepts of self-care and compassion, and in the first chapter of part 3, we discussed the first step to self-acceptance, mindfully tuning in to the present.

In this chapter, we will cover the second step to self-acceptance, which involves noticing the distinct parts of yourself. We want to start to draw your attention to a few new things, the first of which is some of the sneaky ways that self-esteem monsters can work, making it just about impossible to notice them in operation or to allow any new, interesting, or different information to come in.

The second piece we want to work on is the other person in the relationship with the self-esteem monster, and that is YOU. Of course, we know this whole "monster versus you" thing is just a metaphor, but we want to spend a bit of time focusing on the other part of you that notices, observes, and watches all this going on. Like the bit of you that is reading these words right now—not the part saying the words in your head, but the part that is watching you say the words in your head. Get it? If not, no problem. Our challenge is to break this down, make it simple, and better yet, practical.

HOW OUR SELF-ESTEEM MONSTERS WORK

Back in chapter 2, we talked about the notion that our self-stories are always there for good reason. They do a lot of harm and can be extremely self-limiting, but they developed for very important reasons: to help keep us safe, protected, and alive. That's why there is often good value in revisiting our childhoods—it helps us make better sense of what is going on now. Without this knowledge of the origins of our self-stories, it can be extremely hard to separate ourselves from them. They end up just seeming like a fundamental truth about ourselves, rather than something passed on to us that we didn't really want or ask for, but needed to help us survive.

It's a bit like if, as a young child, those around you whose job it was to care for and look after you gave you a magic lamp. Not a shiny, nice one within which a cool genie lived that could grant you amazing wishes, but a nasty, grumpy, smelly monster (sound familiar?). Whenever you got scared, anxious, depressed, or lonely, you did what you do with magic lamps—you polished it and out popped your monster. It had all sorts of helpful advice to give you:

Why do my parents always fight all the time?

"Because you're naughty and don't do as you're told."

Why does my mom get angry at me?

"Because you speak your mind—you should keep quiet."

Why does my dad look like he loves my brother more than me?

"Because you're not as interesting—you need to try harder to impress him."

These are painful answers, but at least the monster helped us makes sense of what was happening—and still does. Crucially, it gives us some tips on what we can do to make the situation better. On and on it goes as we desperately try to make sense of confusing, painful, or traumatizing experiences. We go to our magic lamp, polish it, and out pops our monster, ready to help explain. After a lifetime of this, we don't even realize that we're doing it; it becomes automatic and our monster can control us, just like a puppeteer does with a puppet.

In our adult lives, our monsters operate so slickly that we don't even see the ways that they blinker our vision to nice things, compliments, cool invitations, and new opportunities.

Our monsters can be very skilled at drawing our attention to all the ways in which we've screwed up in our lives while ignoring all the times when things actually have, at the very least, gone okay. Our monsters also have a knack for pulling our attention to the worst-case scenarios and how things could (and probably would) go horribly and terribly wrong.

Check out the list that follows. Even if you're doubtful, we'd like you to consider the possibility that if you've ever found yourself saying these things, this may be your monster in operation:

- Good things never happen to me.
- I'm just unlucky.
- People only compliment me to get something.

- People only hang around me because they feel sorry for me.
- If anyone got to know the real me, they'd run for the hills.
- Everything I touch turns to shit.
- Nothing ever works out for me.

The trick is learning the skill to catch our monsters in operation, which is sometimes not so easy, as monsters can be slippery customers. A big part of being able to do this is to take a step back from all of this.

Here is the matrix again for your viewing pleasure (also available to download at http://www.newharbinger.com/43041). We'd like you to fill this matrix out. The questions are essentially the same, but tilted toward thinking about your self-esteem monster more.

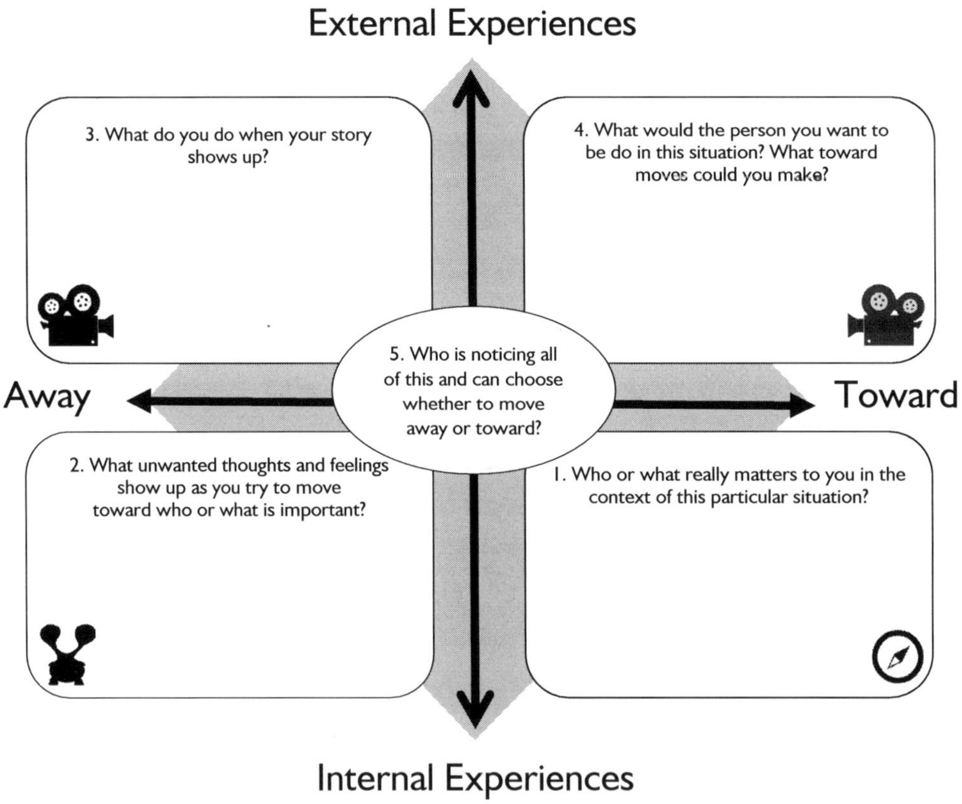

External Experiences

3. What do you do when your story shows up?

4. What would the person you want to be do in this situation? What toward moves could you make?

Away

5. Who is noticing all of this and can choose whether to move away or toward?

Toward

2. What unwanted thoughts and feelings show up as you try to move toward who or what is important?

1. Who or what really matters to you in the context of this particular situation?

Internal Experiences

The question in the middle is the most important question of all: Who is it that's noticing all of this going on and answering all these questions? And no, it's not a trick question—you got it right—of course it's *you* doing all this noticing, watching, and observing!

THE SKY AND THE WEATHER

A favorite quote of ours, widely promoted by Russ Harris (e.g., Harris 2009) and often attributed to the Buddhist teacher Pema Chödrön,* is "You are the sky. Everything else is just weather." This metaphor has two cool aspects. First, it highlights the part of ourselves that is constant, stable, and unchanging. Just as the sky acts to hold and contain all the weather that passes through, from the gentlest of breezes to the mightiest of hurricanes, no matter what raging emotion, screaming monster, or gloomy feeling is present, that part of us that holds and contains all these experiences will be there. It will be there to observe the next change to come along, whatever that might be. Which brings us to the second part: the metaphor helps us to remember that our experience is ever changing. It's perhaps the only constant, that we're always changing. This helps to promote a sense of detachment when our self-esteem monsters stomp about like they own the place and are here to stay. That observer part acts as a quiet reminder that this shall pass. It also reminds us that when we have brilliant sunshine, rays of hope, and glorious happiness and are filled with bulletproof confidence, this too shall pass. Occupying this observer place reminds us not to struggle with or cling too tightly to these parts of our experience. Everything is transient.

The heart of this message is that this part of ourselves acts a bit like a container for all of our experiences. Admittedly, at times, it can feel like our TEAMS *have us,* rather than us having them. We'd like to do an exercise that seeks to strengthen this notion of us, or our sense of I, as the container of all our experiences.

---

* Although this quotation is widely attributed to Pema Chödrön, it does not appear in any of her writings. We contacted the Pema Chödrön Foundation, who told us that the author herself could not recall the origin of the quote.

OBSERVING EXERCISE

(adapted from McHugh, Stewart, and Almada 2019)

Use the outline of the human body below to practice observing different parts of your experience as they occur. You'll need a pen or pencil to do this exercise. (Both the body outline and an audio recording are available at http://www.newharbinger.com/43041.)

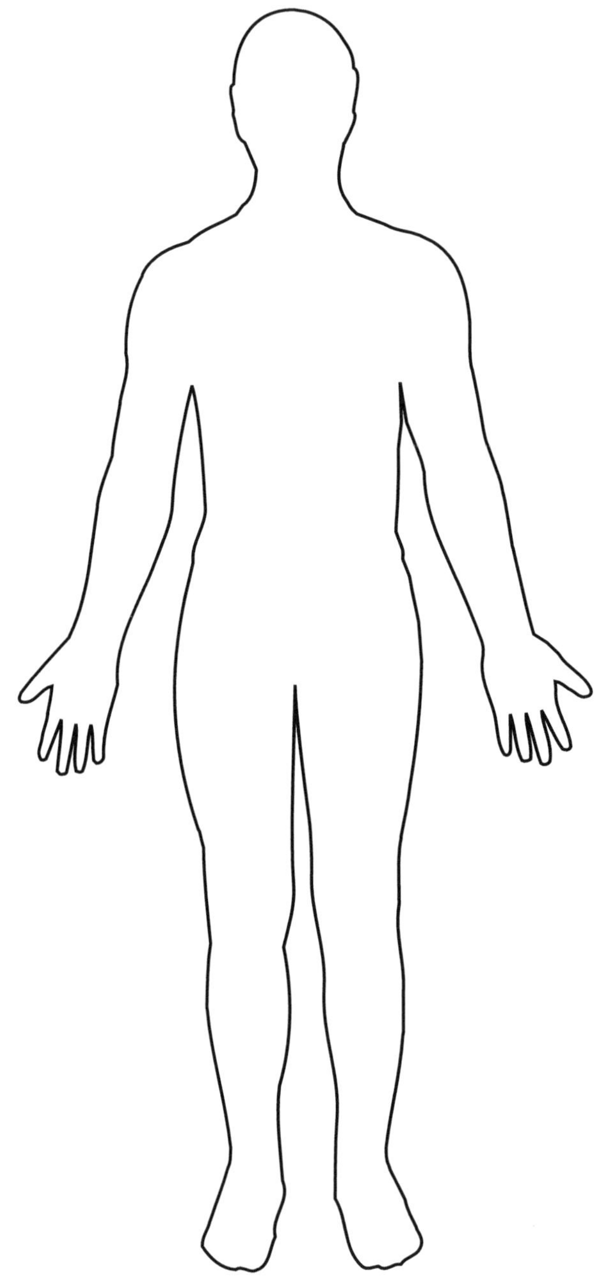

Find a comfy and relatively quiet place to sit. First, allow your attention to notice the sensations of sitting in the chair you're in, just simply observing without changing them. Allow your attention to gather around your breath as you gradually find your awareness settling into the moment. If your attention wanders, that's perfectly fine—just bring it back to noticing in this moment. The task here is to simply notice physical sensations as they occur in your body. See if you can do it without an agenda to change them. As you notice each one, take your pen and place an "X" roughly on the body map, indicating where the sensation occurred. Take a minute or so to observe any sensations as they occur, and mark them on the body map.

And now, we're going to move to emotions. Bring your awareness to wherever in your body you notice your emotions. As you notice an emotion, take your pen and mark "O" on the body map for where you felt the emotion. It doesn't have to be perfect, and if you don't notice anything, that's fine. Take another minute to notice any emotions that arrive.

We are now going to move on to thoughts. Bring your awareness to your mind and thoughts. As you notice a thought come to mind, write it in a speech bubble next to the diagram of your body. It doesn't have to be exactly what you were thinking—just as close as possible. Take another minute to do so.

So, there you were, noticing sensations, emotions, and thoughts. If we were to give this part of you a name, we'd call it the Observing Self. It's not made up of all the sensations, emotions, and thoughts, but it's the part of you that holds them all and observes them.

Lastly, we'd like you to bring to mind an experience you went through some months ago—perhaps something you found enjoyable. See if you can drop yourself back into the memory and look out from behind your own eyes. What can you sense? What emotions are present? What thoughts are there with you? See if you can remember these experiences as you did when you were there. There you were then, noticing and being aware of all these experiences. And notice that you are here, noticing yourself noticing all these experiences. Although the thoughts, sensations, and emotions are all different, see if you can connect in a way with how that part of you that noticed then is the same you that notices now. And that part of you that notices is that part of you that has just about always been there, throughout your whole life. Not your ever-changing thoughts, emotions, and sensations, but the part of you that notices, observes, and chooses.

Take some time now to make some notes below on your thoughts and experiences:

____

____

____

CHANGE, THE ONLY CONSTANT

Both of us nostalgically remember the old box of photos that we had growing up that got dragged out at family gatherings. We all got to laugh at the dodgy haircuts and fashion, and how back then we never thought we'd ever end up looking so uncool. Little did we know. But these days, most of us carry our photos around in a camera roll on our phones. Which leads us neatly to our next metaphor. If you're like us, you have hundreds of photos on your phone representing all sorts of events, occasions, and situations. Now all of these images are like the vast array of TEAMS that we have over our lifetime, and these experiences are all contained within something, and that is our phone or device. This device is the container that holds the experiences, but it is not the experiences themselves. It contains them, and yet it is separate from them. More photos might get added or deleted, but the containing device remains the same.

There's a special point we want to make here from this metaphor. If there is one absolute certainty here, it's that everything will change. All our TEAMS constantly move through us. Hundreds of thousands, if not millions, over our lifetimes. Think of all the experiences you've forgotten! Remembering what we had for lunch three days ago is tough enough, let alone all the rest of the far more important material that's been lost to time. This is where it's important to consider one of the ways our self-esteem monsters work. They like a nice, simple, coherent narrative about you. Anything that doesn't fit the story, well, that gets thrown out. Coherent means safe and predictable, so it's understandable that this happens, even if it's incredibly limiting at times.

We have another exercise for you to do. This won't necessarily be easy, but we'd like you to give it your best shot.

NEW EXPERIENCES

We'd like you to gather together experiences you can remember that fall outside of what your self-esteem monster would have you believe about yourself or what you could do. It could be things that you go back through your memory for. Or it could be things that you make a note to remember over the week. The point here is not to challenge the monster, or prove it wrong, or make this an "everything is awesome!" exercise. It's just to show that there are other perspectives available.

To help you out, below is an example of how someone completed this exercise.

New Experiences Worksheet

What memories do you have that fall outside what your monster would have you remember?	What qualities, strengths, abilities, or talents do you have that your monster doesn't like to recognize?	What actions have you taken in your life that your monster did not think you would be able to do?	What things do other people say about you that don't fit with all the things your monster says about you?	What would an older, wiser, kinder you, looking back on yourself now, notice about you that the monster can't see about you?
Sitting by the river, watching the fish jump and feeling so calm. *Being at the music festival and getting lost but meeting that girl who helped me and had a laugh with me.*	*I'm good at empathizing.* *I have a weird sense of humor.* *I'm a creative dancer.*	*That one time I told my dad to leave me alone, even though I was so scared.* *That I dropped out of college and went traveling alone for 6 months.* *That I decided to study graphic design at the university.*	*I'm kind.* *I speak my mind.* *I cry easily.* *I'm not fake, I'm authentic.*	*You miss the bigger picture of you. You're more than a one-dimensional cartoon. You're not perfect, by any stretch, but you're actually an OK person, a pretty decent one, in fact.*

Now you take a stab at it. There's a good chance this exercise will feel very weird. You may notice thoughts like *That's not me,* or *I'm just pretending; I'm a fraud,* or *This is just going to make things worse, setting myself up for a fall.* Just notice these thoughts and keep open to the possibility that they reflect the voice of your monster, kicking up a stink. Then fill in the New Experiences Worksheet below, which is also available at http://www.newharbinger.com/43041.

New Experiences Worksheet

What memories do you have that fall outside what your monster would have you remember?	What qualities, strengths, abilities, or talents do you have that your monster doesn't like to recognize?	What actions have you taken in your life that your monster did not think you would be able to do?	What things do other people say about you that don't fit with all the things your monster says about you?	What would an older, wiser, kinder you, looking back on yourself now, notice about you that the monster can't see about you?

MORE THAN ONE SELF-STORY

Throughout most of this book, we've talked about self-stories and self-esteem monsters as if we have only one. Being a metaphor, of course, we hold this lightly, which is to say that we humans can have a lot going on and different versions of unhelpful self-stories that operate in a similar way. For example, a person might have a monster that tells them they're a failure because they haven't achieved enough in life. They may have another version that says they're unlovable because underneath it all they're a dirty and disgusting human being. At their heart, both stories are saying that the person doesn't measure up in some basic and fundamental way.

There is a somewhat different way that this can occur; this is when two self-stories develop alongside each other, in tandem. There are two main ways this happens.

The vulnerable and overprotector relationship. The vulnerable self-story develops when a person has missed out on receiving key love, care, and affection growing up and, starved of this, reaches out to others in desperate and sometimes uncontained or unsafe ways. This could mean charging headlong into relationships, pushing friendships too quickly, or bending over backward to be liked and being a people pleaser who quickly gets taken advantage of.

Therefore, it's quite common for another self-story to develop: the overprotector. The protector's job is to do everything it can to shut down the vulnerable side and stop it from entering into unsafe situations. This can mean limiting or disconnecting from relationships, working excessively hard to be independent, and making sure the person doesn't come to rely on anyone. And it can mean being incredibly harsh, critical, and nasty toward the needy side. Sometimes, taken to its full extent, this can turn into full-blown self-hatred. As you could imagine, these two self-stories look very different from one another, and the relationship between the two can sometimes be extremely antagonistic.

The self-blame and victim relationship. The second way tandem self-stories can play out is when one self-story takes excessive responsibility for the harm and damage that was caused to them growing up. This can cause a lot of undue pain, but it has an often unseen bonus of internally locating the responsibility for change. People will say to themselves, *It was my fault; I should have been smarter/better/funnier/quieter. If I were different, then I wouldn't be in this mess.* Sometimes a very different self-story can develop alongside this, which firmly locates responsibility for harm externally and with the actual people (e.g., family, caregivers) who perpetrated the harm. With this can come very high levels of understandable anger toward those people. But along with this, the place for change gets located outside of the person, which can lead to powerlessness in the face of strong emotions or unhelpful behaviors.

These two aspects then go to battle with each other. One says, *I'm to blame but that means I can change!* The other says, *There is no way I am to blame; I'm the victim here, I did nothing wrong—they need to accept responsibility before anything changes!* When you step back far enough, you can see there are grains of truth in each of these perspectives.

If you've ever experienced this kind of scenario, it can be incredibly destabilizing, and you may find it hard to know what to think and feel, or even to trust yourself. Two parts of yourself battle it out, and the part of you we were referring to earlier, the Observing Self, becomes very small.

When they are battling each other, it becomes extraordinarily hard to answer the question, "Given all that I've been through, what kind of person do I want to be?" This isn't a question that is going to be usefully answered from the perspective of just one side. That is likely to only engender a further battle. What's needed is a place where both perspectives can be acknowledged, heard, and brought together. That place is from the observer perspective.

TWO SIDES TALKING

Take out a pen and paper and answer the following questions:

To begin with, give the first side of the paper a name. Choose the one that sits right for you. Here are our suggestions: "I'm bad/broken," "I deserved it," "I'm weak," "I'm vulnerable."

And from the perspective of that side, answer the following questions:

- What are the most important feelings that I need heard and recognized?
- What are the important experiences I've been through that need to be remembered?
- What are my weaknesses and vulnerabilities?
- What worries and concerns me the most?
- What are my strengths?
- What, deep down, is most important to me?

Now, give the second side a name, for example, "Victim," "Protector," "Anger." And now, from the perspective of this side, answer the following questions:

- What are the most important feelings that I need heard and recognized?
- What are the important experiences I've been through that need to be remembered?
- What are my weaknesses and vulnerabilities?
- What worries and concerns me the most?

- What are my strengths?
- What, deep down, is most important to me?

From the place of the Observing Self, we'd like you to take some time and bring both of these perspectives together in a coherent way. Imagine you are a caring parent and you're standing above each side. You're going to gather up both of these sides together in your arms, listen to them, value their perspectives, and decide from that place how you're going to act. Given each of these perspectives, their differences, their strengths and their weaknesses, what kind of person do you want to be? Take a moment to make some notes below:

____

____

____

____

____

We know we've been talking throughout this book about doing what matters, knowing what's important, and acting on your values. If you're one of those people who just goes, "I haven't got an f-ing clue what my values are," don't worry—we will come to this topic in chapter 11. We appreciate that it's a BIG topic.

IN SUMMARY

There are a few things we'd like you to catch from this chapter. First of all, there's you and then there's your self-esteem monster or self-story. In the metaphor, we've made the point that these two parts of you are distinct. Here's the next thing to catch: your experiences (TEAMS) vary tremendously, as do your beliefs about yourself and your place in the world. Your self-esteem monster (and let's be honest, you too) quite likes a bit of stability and for things to just be simple and make sense. But you are a more complex organism that can't be boiled down to a simple statement. There is this other part of you that isn't made up of all this stuff—it's the part that observes all these changes and therefore has this unique noticing, observing perspective. It's stable and has been there your whole life, the consistent part of you.

One final point: this observing perspective is not dispassionate or passive. It's like a big container that holds everything. Like the sky that holds the weather. And your monster, big and ugly, strong and protective as it is, is just another part of all of this ever-changing, fluid, moving, evolving, dynamic stuff. Cool, right? So we want to be a little cautious about getting into battles with our monsters because they are, well, just parts of ourselves. What if we could do something radically different and learn to accept and love ourselves, and our monsters, warts and all? This leads us nicely to our next chapter, where we'll cover the third step to self-acceptance—making room for your thoughts and feelings.

Bringing It All Together

As you pause and reflect again at the end of this chapter, take a moment to bring together your thoughts and impressions on what you've just read. What were the parts that resonated with you?

____

____

Think about your relationship with your self-esteem monster as it stands now. What difference does it make to think about the observer part of you and your monster?

____

____

CHAPTER 9

Making Room

Monsters. Not the kind of characters you would usually want to make room for. The very word makes most of us want to think about either running and hiding or gearing up for a fight. Because with all the potential pain and misery of difficult self-stories that we've talked about so far, fight and flight seem like obvious solutions, and there are many different ways we tend to do that. This chapter will go through some of the reasons why consistently fighting or running away from thoughts and feelings about ourselves might not always be the best strategy, and how doing the exact opposite of what comes naturally—that is, making room for these thoughts and feelings—might lead us closer to the life we really want.

AVOIDANCE: THE GOOD, THE BAD, AND THE UGLY

To make this chapter easier to read, we are going to group a wide range of behaviors together, under the term "avoidance." It's going to mean all of those things that humans do to try and turn the volume down on the thoughts and feelings that they don't like. Avoidance is as old as the hills. It's a natural response to a threat. All of Earth's creatures do it in some form or another, whether it's a snail retreating into its shell or a mouse running away from a cat. There's nothing intrinsically wrong with it, and sometimes it's even helpful, as we'll discuss below. When facing a threat in the external world, running away makes absolute sense. The problems start to arise when the threat comes from inside our heads and we get stuck using the same strategy.

In our experience, self-related thoughts like *I'm no good* are way up there in terms of the internal stuff we habitually want to run from. Just think for a moment: when your monster is giving you a hard time, what do you do to try and get rid of it or quiet it down? Do you actively try and defeat it or just quietly submit to what it says and hope it goes away, satisfied that it's got you under its control? Typical avoidance strategies include things like withdrawing from other people, distracting ourselves by just "keeping busy," overworking, using drugs and alcohol, and self-harm. While these behaviors might look very different on the surface, they all serve the same function of trying not to feel so bad.

If you recognize that sometimes you adopt a strategy of avoidance as a way of dealing with your monster, make a note here of the things that you most frequently do.

___

___

___

___

The first thing we want to be absolutely clear on, which hopefully you will remember from completing the matrix, is that sometimes avoidance can be a good and helpful thing. Constantly being in touch with painful self-stories is probably not workable. Most people like the occasional "night on the town" or "duvet day" in order to get away from the stresses and strains of life. If nothing else, it works, at least in the sense of buying you some temporary respite. We only ever do anything because it works for us in some way. So, if you sometimes make use of avoidant behaviors, we would be the last people to give you a hard time about that, and we wouldn't want you to do that either. What we would like you to consider, though, is the cost of doing so, and here's where we get into the bad side of avoiding the monster. Try out the exercise below in order to start exploring the costs of avoidance.

THE MONSTER MANUAL

Just for a few minutes, imagine that this book is no longer a self-acceptance workbook. Imagine it is your monster's own personal handbook on how to bring you down. It is full of all the negative, derogatory stories that have come into your mind through the years. It is the ultimate resource pack for your monster in the task of making you feel terrible about yourself. Naturally, this is not a manual that you want to read. You don't want it near you. What we would like you to do is lift your pretend monster manual up and hold the awful thing as far away from you as you can, arms outstretched, way out in front of you. Get as much distance between you and the book as possible, without actually putting it down. Keep pushing it away for a couple of minutes and don't slack off. Just when you think you couldn't put any more effort into pushing it away, push it away that little bit more.

What do you notice as you do this? Maybe you feel silly. Maybe your arms feel tired. Maybe, despite your efforts to push this horrible thing away, there it is still in your hands—it hasn't really gone anywhere. You are trying to avoid it. Is it working? What would it be like if you spent the rest of the day like this? How tired would you become? How much would pushing the monster manual away interfere with other things you have planned for the day? What might you miss out on? What other costs might there be?

Okay, now you can relax and put it down in front of you. Just let it and all its nasty content sit there, without trying hard to get away from it. What do you notice now? Is putting it down easier, or do you wish you were still pushing it away?

If you wish, you can make a few notes about what you noticed below.

____

____

____

____

There are a few important things to catch from the above exercise. First, avoidant behavior *can* help create some distance between you and all the difficult stuff in any good monster manual, like self-doubt or self-criticism. Second, doing so comes at a cost, in that if you put all your energy into avoidance, there are other things you will be much less able to do. Third, ask yourself what the difference was between the experience of pushing the book away and the experience of just letting it sit there in front of you. Which of those types of experiences would you like to have more of in your life? Essentially, this is the choice between avoidance and acceptance. Finally, we would invite you to consider how you might respond if you were invited to hold a monster manual belonging to someone you care about. Bring to mind someone you love. Now, imagine for a moment that you stumbled across their monster manual. As you peak inside, you realize it's filled with all the hurtful and painful things their monster says to them. Do you think you would push it away, or would you hold it with kindness and compassion? If it's too hard to think about this from within the monster manual metaphor, just think about a time when someone you care about shared something painful with you, or how you would like someone to respond if you took that same brave step and shared something painful with them. Does it feel like an avoidant response or an accepting response was or would be the most helpful?

To summarize this section on avoidance, it is important to acknowledge its occasional utility as a strategy for dealing with uncomfortable experiences. That's the good. On the flip side, using avoidance tends to come at a cost, often in terms of not being able to pursue the things in life that really matter. That's the bad. The ugly is when difficult internal stuff, like pervasively negative self-stories, seems to be so compelling that avoidance in all its forms becomes a default option, and life gets increasingly smaller and less meaningful. It is when the pursuit of almost everything that matters is sacrificed in the service of trying to keep the monster quiet.

Think of it like this. Let's suppose we could offer you the best psychiatric medication ever. This tablet would put an end to everything that troubles your mind. That would mean an end to anxiety, low mood, guilt, shame, and negative thinking. You name it, this tablet would stop it from showing up and bringing you down. Does it sound good so far? And...effective as it is, this tablet, like all medication, has a side effect. The side effect profile of this medication is small. There is only one side effect, and it is that the medication completely paralyzes you so that you cannot move or engage with others. Ask yourself if you would take it if it were offered to you. Would you choose a life of contentment and comfort in bed, free from the hassle of pursuing your goals and values, and swallow that tablet? Or, would you decide that no matter what discomfort might come your way, there are some things that are worth getting out of bed for, and choose not to take it? If you think the latter sounds preferable, read on as we talk some more about how acceptance can transform the relationship we have with our monsters.

THE MONSTER THAT BLOCKS THE DOOR

If there's one thing we like, it's a metaphor. In previous chapters, we used the metaphor of a monster to represent the comprehensive network of thoughts involving self-criticism and judgment. Hopefully, reading this book has helped you to see, name, and understand more about how your monster operates and how you respond to it. Our monsters tend to reflect the accumulated pain from our histories, like grief from past hurts, anger at injustices, or sadness at opportunities lost. They have a habit of storing this stuff up and then telling us that it's our fault. It's no wonder we feel like running away or fighting to overpower them.

One way to look at this is as if the monster is blocking the door to the life that you want, with all that gives it meaning and purpose. The door is the portal to this life, and behind it are all the activities that you enjoy and the rewarding relationships with people you care about. However, the monster knows that there are potential challenges and discomfort behind there, too. It knows, as we all do really, that nothing meaningful comes without a degree of stress and discomfort, for example, building a career or working on maintaining a long-term relationship. As much as you want to go through, the monster wants to protect you, so the two of you get locked in a never-ending struggle. You've come to believe you need to defeat the monster first in order to go through the door (e.g., *I'll ask that person out on a date when I feel better about myself*), and the monster believes that going through it is fraught with danger, so it tries to stop you (e.g., "I can't allow you to risk being rejected by asking people out on dates!").

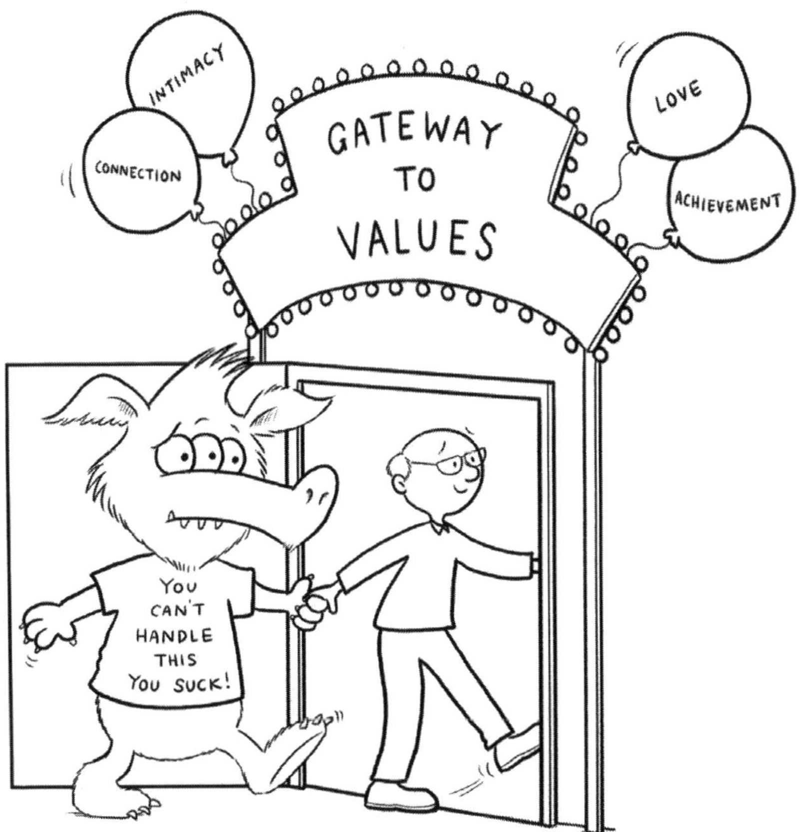

The acceptance move we are proposing here is to drop the struggle with the monster. Maybe it is possible to radically alter your relationship with it. Maybe you could stop fighting it and do something *way* out there…maybe you could take it by the hand and choose to go through the door together. What a team the two of you could make! You, intent on pursuing the things that really matter, with your monster reminding you of the dangers and urging caution. It's probably going to hound you more than you want, and maybe that's a price worth paying for getting to experience everything on the other side of the door. After all, you don't always have to listen if what it says isn't helpful.

Below, we are going to stress the idea that the things that we really care about in life are deeply connected to the hurt we experience. At some level, you probably already know this. For example, we contact grief so as to honor loved ones who have died. We might feel the sadness of how our parents didn't meet our needs so that we can be clearer about how to care for ourselves better. We might allow ourselves to feel anger at injustice so that we can channel that to work at promoting fairness. It is the inextricable link between value and pain.

IN YOUR PAIN YOU FIND YOUR VALUES

If you are reading this book because the topic of low self-esteem resonated with you, there's a good chance that you will know the experience of uncomfortable thoughts and feelings only too well. You will probably have tried all sorts of things to avoid them, believing that you would be better off if this discomfort were eliminated. We want to suggest something different to you, from a place of kindness and acceptance:

You are not broken, and you do not need to be fixed.

Those uncomfortable things you experience, those things that you might think make you different from everyone else, actually connect you to everyone else. The struggle against the monster is probably doing you more harm than just letting it be there would. Of course, it's okay to want to manage difficult thoughts and feelings. All we are saying is don't do it just to "improve your self-esteem" (e.g., changing *I'm completely worthless* into *I'm totally awesome*). Instead, work toward seeing them as evidence of your humanity and toward adopting a kinder view of them, the way you might do if they were the thoughts and feelings of a friend or a loved one. Once there, you can focus on your capacity to take action.

Why would we want you to make room for the difficult stuff? You might reasonably be asking yourself, *What's in this for me?* Often people worry that if they stop fighting the monster and allow the difficult stuff to simply be present, it will be a slippery slope and loads more monsters will show up. Does this really happen? On the contrary, bad things tend to magnify when you try to eliminate them. What you resist persists. When you accept that they are there, they have less of a hold on you. When that happens—when you drop the struggle with your monster and stop the fight to always feel good—you can choose to *do* what matters, rather than trying and failing to *feel* what you want to feel.

Perhaps the biggest problem with trying to avoid the discomfort that comes along with negative self-stories is that much of that discomfort tells us something important about what it is that really matters in life. Within the therapy work we do, there is one notion that comes up over and over again:

In your pain you find your values, and in your values you find your pain.

It feels like one of life's most important messages, and you probably already know it to be right, even if you have never stopped to think about it. As suggested above, we tend to hurt and care in the same places. When we ask our clients about the most important moments of their lives, they invariably mention things like gaining a qualification, bringing up children, surviving an illness, or acquiring a skill. They almost always talk about things that were hard won, and—here's the interesting bit—things that *also* gave rise to enormous amounts of distress and self-criticism. No one ever mentions winning the lottery or inheriting a bunch of money. While they are the kinds of events that would be great, they are not things that require any effort, and therefore they tend to mean less to people. Invariably, the things that matter most are also the things that give us the most opportunity for psychological suffering.

So, if difficult thoughts and feelings are simply the flip side of choosing to value certain things in life, why not drop the struggle with the monster and just let the discomfort be there? Lots of reasons, probably. Perhaps it feels scary or unfamiliar. While stepping outside of your comfort zone is always going to be uncomfortable, practicing self-acceptance better prepares us for dealing with that discomfort. It helps us roll with the punches with more flexibility. It is better preparation for a life well lived than trying to pretend that the positive self-stories are the only ones worth listening to. The key thing is to figure out what really matters to you. Might you be willing to let the monster stick around if it meant that you could pursue this more effectively?

It is easy for us to pose a question about what it is that matters most to you in life. Also, we appreciate that this can be hard to answer sometimes. In keeping with the values/pain idea, just thinking about your values can be painful. So try and approach the exercise below with some self-compassion, and don't give yourself too much of a hard time if it is difficult, or if responses to the values side of it don't come easily. We are really just dipping a toe into the question of values at this stage and will cover it in more depth later in the book.

FINDING THE FLIP SIDE

If you completed the exercise in chapter 3 entitled "The Different Stories in Our Heads," you will have identified three dominant negative self-stories. Based on the idea of values and pain being two sides of the same coin, we would like you to revisit these three sentences to try to identify what these stories might be telling you about what it is that really matters. One way to go about this is to ask yourself what you would need to give up caring about in order to guarantee that the negative self-story never bothered you.

Here are a few completed examples from our own experience to give you a sense of what we mean.

Negative self-story	What this says about what I care about
I am *selfish.*	*I care about other people's needs.*
I am *boring.*	*I want other people to enjoy my company.*
I am *a huge letdown.*	*I want to do right by other people.*

Hopefully you can see from these examples that the act of caring about something goes some way to explaining the presence of the negative self-story (e.g., If I didn't ever care about the needs of other people, I would probably never even think about whether I was selfish or not). Now go ahead and try this exercise for yourself using the three negative self-stories from the earlier exercise.

Negative self-story	What this says about what I care about
I am	
I am	
I am	

CHOOSING ACCEPTANCE

The word "acceptance" can have a passive connotation, and it might feel like defeat or just waving a white flag while life rolls you over. We tend not to think of it like this and instead see it as an active choice. We are not recommending getting better at acceptance because we want to see you suffer. Rather, we are doing so because we have seen many of our clients transform their lives by choosing to give up the struggle with their negative self-stories. If you are reading this book, you probably know suffering already. Our belief is that much of that suffering is made worse through pursuing an avoidance agenda. Here's another tidy one-liner for you to consider:

The problem isn't the problem—the solution is the problem.

If you haven't thrown the book across the room in frustration at this point, well done. We really appreciate your persistence. What this sentence suggests is that negative self-stories are actually less of an issue than all the things we do to try and reduce their influence, such as avoidance. Don't take our word for it. Complete the exercise below and decide for yourself.

PROBLEMS AND SOLUTIONS

Take an aspect or two of your negative self-story and write it down below under "Problem." Then, opposite that, list all of the things you do to try and get away from it or turn down the volume on it. Here are a few examples from our clients' experience to give you a sense of what we mean.

Problem	Solutions I have tried
I am *a huge letdown.*	*Go out of my way to do whatever other people want in order to feel worthwhile* *Keep busy and try to block the thought* *Drink alcohol to numb myself out* *Ignore phone calls from friends* *Self-harm to punish myself*

Now try this exercise for yourself, following the example above.

Problem	Solutions I have tried
I am	

With reference to the above exercise, if we could go back in time and offer you a choice of (a) a life with that problematic self-story or (b) a life with that problematic self-story *and* all of your solutions and their consequences, which do you think you would choose? Has all the avoidance and struggling with the monster been the better option? Has it helped? Have the costs been worth the benefits? Only you will know the answers.

Here's another exercise to help you think about whether acceptance might be better for you when the monster shows up.

THE TWO SIDES OF THE PAPER

Take a blank piece of paper. On one side, write a typical thing that your negative self-story says is true about you—something that might be difficult to hear and painful to acknowledge. Start it with "I am..."

As with the "Finding the Flip Side" exercise above, think about what this pain might be telling you about what is important. One way to do this is to look at what you have written on the "pain" side of the paper and answer the question, "What would I have to give up caring about in order to never experience this painful thought again?" When you have your answer, write that on the other side of the paper, the "value" side.

Here are some examples:

Pain side	Value side
My self-story says...	What would I have to give up caring about in order to never experience this painful thought again?
I am useless.	*Being useful*
I am too messed up myself to help others.	*Caring for others*
I am unlovable.	*Being loved*

Now take your piece of paper with you and find a trash can. What if we could offer you an easy way out of your pain? All you need to do is rip up the paper and throw it in the trash. The only catch is that you would have to lose the value as well. Ask yourself if you would do it. What might be gained or lost with whatever you decided to do?

We don't know whether you still have your piece of paper or if it's in little pieces with the rest of the trash. If you decided to rip it up, that might mean that the pursuit of that particular value was just not worth the cost of experiencing the pain that came with it. If you still have it, and the value was too important for you to sacrifice, then you have chosen to accept the pain. Maybe you considered that keeping the pain was an acceptable price to pay for also being able to keep the value.

The origin of the word "accept" has links with ideas such as *consenting to receive* and *taking something to oneself,* as in accepting a gift. Our belief is that the biggest gift that acceptance has to offer is that it enables us to more effectively pursue our values. When you are willing to have discomfort *in the service of the things that matter,* taking action that is about "more of the good stuff" can take the place of actions that are all about "less of the bad stuff."

PUTTING ACCEPTANCE INTO ACTION

There is no particular prescription for bringing a quality of acceptance into your life. Broadly speaking, it is about taking steps in the direction that you choose, noticing what shows up when you do so, and allowing those things to be part of the experience without working to control, reduce, or eliminate them. Essentially, it is about exposure to your emotions, allowing yourself to feel whatever you feel, and learning that experiencing difficult thoughts and feelings does not have to be a barrier to doing things that are important to you.

Research has shown that approaching life with an accepting mindset makes potentially difficult activities more achievable, and once people learn that thoughts and feelings do not *have* to be a barrier to acting in the way they want, they are more likely to take further value-driven steps in the future (Swain et al. 2013). The impact of this mindset is maintained in the long term and is strengthened with further practice. If you are devoting less energy to trying to control how you think and feel about yourself, you will have more energy to invest in living life the way you want to. However, your monster is unlikely to come along quietly at first; it might give you a hard time for a good while. We will round out this chapter with a few ideas for strengthening those acceptance muscles, to help you in those moments when your story really gives you a hard time. Here are a few questions to ask of yourself when the going gets tough:

- What is this painful experience telling me about what it is that matters?
- Would trying to accept this discomfort help me or harm me in the long term?
- What might my older, wiser self say that I should do?
- When was the first time this painful thing ever showed up? How old was I back then? What did I look like? What if that younger version of me were here in pain right now? What caring thing could I say to my younger self that might be helpful to them?
- If a close friend came to me with this difficulty, how would I respond? Would I tell them to snap out of it or would I make room for them and their suffering?

- If this were happening to the main character in a movie, what might the message of that movie be? What might they gain or learn from facing the adversity? How might it make them stronger or wiser?

IN SUMMARY

When dealing with the adversity presented by difficult thoughts and feelings, many people fight and struggle with them in order to make them go away or simply try to avoid them. Such strategies can have some short-term benefits, although they don't tend to work out well over the long haul. If we make it a priority to avoid our self-stories, we end up constructing our lives around not feeling bad, rather than around living well. Consistent with this, research has found that adopting an attitude of acceptance can be a more effective strategy. Because the things we most care about are often also the things that give rise to the most hurt, avoiding discomfort also tends to mean avoiding those aspects of life that matter most to us. If we can accept that discomfort is just part of the picture of a life well lived, it enables us to act in line with what really matters to us. Pervasive negative self-stories can be an obstacle to living well, particularly if we get caught up with the idea that the story needs to change before we can start living. We are suggesting that you start living right now and take your monster along for the ride. There's only one way to find out if that will work for you. In the next chapter, we're going to take you through six practical skills that will help you to do this.

Bringing It All Together

Take a moment to consider what you have learned about acceptance from this chapter. Does it seem like a useful alternative to avoidance? If it does, list a few reasons why working on being able to make room for discomfort might be of benefit to you.

____

____

____

____

____

____

CHAPTER 10

Catching Comparisons: Learning the Art of Self-Acceptance

In his play *No Exit,* Jean-Paul Sartre, the French philosopher and writer, places three characters in hell (Sartre [1944] 1989). Hell, it turns out, is not the traditional fire and brimstone, but a simple room in which the characters are subjected to the steady, judging gaze of each other. One of the characters laments, "Hell is other people!" Sartre's point wasn't that everyone is invariably hellish, but rather that we view and judge ourselves by the means that other people have given us for judging ourselves.

This is a good reminder that the way we interact with our self-esteem story is very seldom done quietly alone or in the privacy of our homes. It's done very much in relation to other people. When we consider if we're adequate or good enough, we're comparing our adequacy and worth to that of those around us. For those of us who have self-esteem monsters that are very rehearsed at this comparison game, we seldom come out of this feeling great about ourselves.

EXPLORING OUR TRIGGERS

The dilemma is that Sartre's famous quote can be flipped to "Heaven is other people." The potential of love, acceptance, and connection with other people is incredibly rewarding and meaningful. This can then put us in a painful push-pull situation when we crave human connection but are repelled by it because of the pain that contact with other people causes.

But remember, if being around other people is hard for you, it does not mean you are weird, broken, or damaged. It means that your history of being around others has been painful and difficult, sometimes incredibly so. Like anyone who has experienced hurt and pain, you naturally become wary of cues that remind you of being hurt in the past. It just so happens that being in the presence of other people is now what triggers these cues.

Note that when we say "in the presence of other people," we don't always mean it literally. Often it can be anticipating (going on a first date, planning to ask someone for a favor), remembering (how you felt when you last met your friends, watching a movie and recalling how lonely you sometimes feel), or, of course, pulling out your phone and connecting to the many opportunities for comparison that we call social media.

Most of the time, it's not just being around *anyone at all* that activates our self-esteem story (although sometimes it can be). It is usually specific situations related to being around others that does it. Almost invariably, the kinds of situations that are triggers for you will be related to your particular history. Having said that, here are a few key ones we'd like you to consider. Put a check mark next to any that you relate to:

Your Trigger Situations

☐ Needing to ask someone for a favor

☐ Being criticized by someone

☐ Needing to express displeasure or anger to another person

☐ Saying no to someone

☐ Saying yes to someone

☐ Being confronted about your behavior

☐ Someone expressing anger toward you

☐ Needing to open up and be vulnerable

☐ Someone telling you about something good that happened to them

☐ Receiving a compliment from someone

☐ Being around people who are physically attractive

☐ Being around people who are talented

☐ Others? ____

In the face of such triggers, your self-esteem monster comes charging out of its box, looking to compare you to this other person. Of course, your monster doesn't do this in a reasonable, balanced way. It goes into this process with all its preconceptions about who you are, based on the old stories you've learned about yourself, and makes sure you don't consider any positive or even neutral perspectives. Inevitably, this comparison leaves you coming out as defective, not good enough, useless, weak, or in some way *less* than the person you are interacting with or thinking about.

When this happens, one option is to succumb to this process and go along with everything that your monster is saying about you and the other person. In this case, you agree with the monster so as not to cause a fuss and then act in accordance with it. Here are some common examples. Put a check mark next to the ones you recognize you do:

Ways I Bring Myself Down

- ☐ Actively putting myself down
- ☐ Putting other people on a pedestal
- ☐ Removing myself from the situation
- ☐ Giving in
- ☐ Keeping quiet
- ☐ Squashing my feelings
- ☐ Convincing myself that I'm wrong or my view is not important
- ☐ Avoiding difficult or challenging situations
- ☐ Others? ______________________________

Of course, these are effective, at least in the sense that they keep your monster quiet, and this feels good in the short term. But there is a significant price to pay in that the status quo is maintained and what you want or need doesn't get heard.

Another strategy is to go completely in the opposite direction. Instead of bringing yourself down, you tear the other person down. Here's a list of some of the popular strategies. Again, put a check mark next to the ones you find yourself engaging in:

Ways I Bring Others Down

- ☐ Criticizing the other person
- ☐ Gossiping behind the other person's back
- ☐ Making lists of the ways I am better than them
- ☐ Telling the other person about only my strengths and minimizing my vulnerabilities
- ☐ Acting in cold or distant ways toward the other person
- ☐ Gaslighting (subtly undermining the other person's beliefs)
- ☐ Withholding praise or positive feedback
- ☐ Belittling the other person's opinions
- ☐ Others? ______________________________

There is a good chance that these strategies work in that they may make you feel better in the short term. If you manage to bring someone down, then you might feel superior or more powerful in relation to them, at least for a while. However, therein lies one of the problems with this strategy: it tends not to be long lasting and works only until the next trigger comes along. The second problem is that these types of strategies are not great for forming long-lasting, supportive relationships with others. They tend to corrode relationships and can leave you feeling even more isolated.

Having said all that, just as we discussed in chapter 9 in terms of avoidance, we would argue that there is nothing inherently wrong with either succumbing to the monster or going on the attack. It is human to give in to negative comparisons of ourselves, and it is human to want to criticize others to make ourselves feel better. It's just that while these strategies dominate and your monster is bossing you around, a bigger question gets obscured: when difficult situations pull you to compare yourself to other people, **how would you want to act if you could choose?**

SIX HABITS OF HIGHLY ACCEPTING PEOPLE

We will offer you six key strategies to help you get out of the trap of comparisons and criticism and help you develop skills so you can choose the actions consistent with the kind of person you want to be.

Comparison Spotting

The very first thing we want you to get good at is spotting your comparisons in action. In our experience, most people are pretty good at knowing when they are comparing themselves to others. What we want you to notice is not just the comparison itself. We want you to get good at stepping back so you can observe the whole process in action.

Here's one thing to say straight away. Although your instinct might be to just simply stop comparing yourself to other people, we're actually not going to ask you to do that. This is because, first of all, if it were that simple, you probably would have done it by now. Second, comparing ourselves to others is about as instinctual as it gets. It would be like asking you to stop looking out for cars when you cross the street. Comparing ourselves is our way of checking to make sure our status in our social group is okay and we're not about to get thrown out. When you think about people who are oblivious to how they are acting in a group, you know how problematic that can be.

Getting eyes on this process is the key to making effective and lasting changes. Here are five things in the process we'd like you to watch out for:

Triggers—What situations do comparisons occur in? With what kind of people? When do they occur? Where are you normally?

Thoughts and Feelings—What thoughts initially emerge about yourself and/or other people? Describe the feelings that arise in the situation. What memories of past experiences bubble up?

Your Monster—What does your monster say about you and how you're feeling? What criticisms or judgments does it make? What does it remind you of? What does it tell you about the future?

Avoidance Pattern—What do you do to quiet the monster down? Do you go along with what the monster says? Do you avoid anything or anyone? Do you blame, judge, or criticize other people?

Impact—What was the effect of your response? How did you feel? In what ways was it useful? Did it help you be the kind of person you want to be or move you further away?

Below is a chart we'd like you to use to begin to track this process. We suggest that you download and print copies of this worksheet, available at http://www.newharbinger.com/43041. Each time you notice comparisons kick in, make some notes in the chart. But first, read through Mark's examples so you get a sense of what we mean.

COMPARISON SPOTTING WORKSHEET

Triggers—What situations do comparisons occur in?	Thoughts and Feelings—What thoughts, feelings, or memories arise in the situation?	Your Monster—What does your monster say about you and how you're feeling?	Avoidance Pattern—What do you do to quiet the monster down?	Impact— What was the effect of your response? What was helpful? What was unhelpful?
A junior colleague told me she's got an interview for the post I applied for	*Sinking feeling, lonely, images of being excluded*	*"This always happens to you. You let this happen to yourself because you're weak."*	*Brag to colleague about how qualified I am for role. Gossip about her to other colleagues*	*Initially feel more in control and then feel I've let myself down a bit*
Out for a drink with a friend who tells me his band has landed their first gig	*Feel anxious and think I should be doing more with my life. A memory of being held back a year at school while all my friends progressed*	*"You're so boring, no one wants to be with you. You're going to end up alone."*	*Stay up until 3 a.m. researching interesting groups I could join*	*Researching made me feel like I was sorting out the problem. But then I felt more depressed as I couldn't be bothered following through on the groups.*

Take some time to complete the worksheet below for yourself.

COMPARISON SPOTTING WORKSHEET

Triggers—What situations do comparisons occur in?	*Thoughts and Feelings*—What thoughts, feelings, or memories arise in the situation?	*Your Monster*—What does your monster say about you and how you're feeling?	*Avoidance Pattern*—What do you do to quiet the monster down?	*Impact*—What was the effect of your response? What was helpful? What was unhelpful?

Having completed the worksheet a number of times, look over your responses to see if you can observe any patterns emerging. The following questions will help you identify patterns.

In what kinds of situations are you most likely to engage in comparisons?

____

____

What are your typical responses that tell you comparisons are happening?

____

____

What does your monster usually say?

____

____

What are your usual responses to your monster? How effective are these responses, in both the short term and the long term?

____

____

Now that you've begun to get a handle on the patterns of your comparisons, we want to move on to the next skill: time traveling.

Time Traveling

When we get stuck comparing ourselves to other people, it's easy to forget that what we are doing has history. This is not the first time we are doing this, and it likely won't be the last. But remembering the history behind what we are doing is often the very thing that allows us to be liberated from it. When we forget our history completely, we are compelled to repeat it because we respond to the triggers as if it's the first time we've encountered them, rather than something we have encountered many times before. We'd like you to take some time to think about a particular situation that has triggered comparisons and see if you can identify any ways it reminds you of your past.

LINKS TO THE PAST

Answer the questions below, using the examples as a guide.

How does this situation remind me of my past?

Ruby said: *Feeling upset in front of other people reminds me of when my dad died and I couldn't tell anyone how I felt because my mom was having a breakdown.*

Your answer:

___

___

___

When else have I felt the feelings I am experiencing now?

Bradley said: *When my partner doesn't listen to me, I feel small, just like I used to when my parents criticized me.*

Your answer:

___

___

___

Who does the person in the current situation remind me of in my past?

Terry said: *When my boyfriend questions my motives, I doubt myself, like when my uncle made me think the abuse wasn't really happening.*

Your answer:

___

___

___

As you make these links between what you are experiencing now and what you have experienced in your past, what conclusions do you draw? If you were able to respond to the present situation on its own terms (and not in terms of the past), what might you do?

Remember that when a plant doesn't grow, we don't blame the plant for being faulty and defective. We look to the soil or lack of water or fertilizer to understand why it didn't thrive. It's for this reason that it's useful to remember the connections between our current struggles and our past. It helps us to respond to ourselves with kindness and understanding.

Reminding Yourself "I Am Here"

Sometimes when we get hooked into comparisons, we end up feeling small, weak, and powerless. At the same time, the other person looms large over us. It's then no wonder that we work very hard to avoid confrontation, keep the peace, or just go along with what the other person wants. We become very focused on not wanting to upset the person or make them angry: we just want to *please* them. Our own needs can then become very small and unimportant. Or, put another way, the other person's needs become our needs. Sound familiar?

It's usually at this point that well-meaning friends and family will say things like "Stand up for yourself!" or "Just do what is best or right for you." Of course, this is good practical advice (and chapters 11 and 12 will help you with exactly that), but an important step is needed first—remembering to stand back and separate yourself from the other person. This is to remind yourself that *you* are *here* and the *other person* is over *there.*

Here are some steps we'd like you to practice to help you do this:

1. Slow down, step out of autopilot mode, and tune in to your body (like you practiced in chapter 7).
2. Take two or three mindful breaths to help you arrive in your body.
3. Remind yourself, *I am here and there you are over there. We are separate and different people.*
4. With kindness, as acknowledging this can be a difficult question, ask yourself, *What do I want in this situation? What is important to me? What do I need?* Let how you are feeling offer you guidance on this question.

Practicing these steps helps you to disentangle yourself from others around you and learn to listen to what you want and need.

Stretching Rubber Bands (Practicing New Behaviors)

Most of us respond in habitual and automatic ways when we engage in comparisons. We end up compromising important parts of ourselves or working to bring the other person down. All of this is to help us feel better or manage uncomfortable emotions. As a result, doing something different or more helpful can often be difficult because we have to give up that way of making ourselves feel better in the short term. Practicing more helpful behaviors is a bit like *stretching a rubber band.* A new rubber band is tight and doesn't have a lot of give, but when we stretch it out repeatedly, it gradually expands and becomes much more flexible and supple. New behavior patterns work in much the same way—initially they can feel awkward or a little restrictive. Over time, as you practice more and more, you will develop more flexibility, and it will become easier to choose how you want to respond, rather than responding how your monster wants you to.

We would like to invite you to consider three new behaviors you would like to practice on a regular basis. To do this, look back through your Comparison Spotting Worksheet from earlier in the chapter and take note of some of your usual ways of responding to situations that invite comparisons. Then, think about some specific actions that are new, different, and potentially more helpful. The trick is not to do the "right" action, just something that will stretch your rubber band out. Here are a few examples:

Jeremy's old behavior: "Gossiping about people who made me feel small"

Jeremy's new behavior: "Giving that person a genuine compliment"

Jeremy's specific action: "Tell my friend's partner that I like his sense of humor"

Suchi's old behavior: "Automatically brushing off positive feedback and discounting it"

Suchi's new behavior: "Whenever someone gives me positive feedback, just saying thank you"

Suchi's specific action: "Over the next week, I will just say thank you three times when people give me nice feedback and I'll make a note each time it happens"

Neeshma's old behavior: "Putting myself down in front of other people"

Neeshma's new behavior: "When opportunities arise, let others know about things I have done well or am proud of"

Neeshma's specific action: "In my job interview next week, make sure I tell the interviewers three positive qualities I have"

Your task is to think of three old behaviors you'd like to change. Then write down what a brand new behavior would look it. Finally, make a note of a specific action you could do over the next two to three weeks that would be in line with this behavior, and practice these behaviors whenever possible. You can download this worksheet at http://www.newharbinger.com/43041.

RUBBER BANDS RECORDING WORKSHEET

My Old Behavior	My New Behavior	Specific Actions

Once you have completed these actions, take some time to reflect on what it was like. How did you find the process of carrying out these actions? What was difficult? What was easy? What have you learned about yourself? What would you like to do more of going forward?

____

____

____

Thanking Your Monster

You've done well sticking with us this far. We know this work is not easy, and we also know it's vital for a healthy, nurturing relationship with yourself and others. We think you might be ready to take it to the next level—what we like to call "black belt compassion skills." Are you ready? We'd now like you to turn your newfound compassion skills toward your self-esteem monster. Eek!

We hope by now you can see why we're suggesting this. Your monster does indeed have sharp claws and teeth. It is pretty scary at times...and, your monster is there for good reason and is not your enemy. It represents an important part of you and your history. As such, we are going to ask you to offer some gratitude, kindness, and warmth to your monster.

But first, let's revisit Mark and see what he wrote:

THANKING MY MONSTER

I'd like to recognize the hard work my monster does, including... *alerting me to dangerous or exposing situations, helping me to remember how things haven't worked out and learn from mistakes, trying to protect me from being hurt in relationships.*

I'd like to thank my monster for... *keeping me safe when I was growing up. It helped me make sense of some confusing experiences and kept me alive. It also helps me to remember all the difficult times I went through growing up and reminds me that it's OK not to be perfect. I'd like to thank it for being persistent in drawing my attention to my pain. Without it I would never have learned to really take care of myself.*

I'd like to extend a hand of warmth and compassion to my monster in the following ways... *in thanking my monster, I want to make a commitment to be kind toward it and the parts of myself that it represents. That doesn't mean I will always listen to it or do what it wants, but I will do my best to be warm toward it by practicing kindness toward even the worst parts of myself.*

Now, take some time to complete these prompts yourself.

THANKING MY MONSTER

I'd like to recognize the hard work my monster does, including…

I'd like to thank my monster for…

I'd like to extend a hand of warmth and compassion to my monster in the following ways…

Gratitude Journaling

In the same way that tapping into your sense of yourself as a "you" that is larger than the negative thoughts you have makes those negative thoughts less absolute and powerful, remembering things in your life for which you feel grateful can make the experience of your self-esteem stories less harsh. When we are locked into comparing ourselves to others and our self-esteem monster is in full flight, criticizing us, putting us down, and generally making us feel pretty terrible about ourselves, it is incredibly easy to forget about the good things in life that we might be grateful for. We'd like you to take some time to consider those things in your life for which you feel grateful and start keeping a journal of these things. The exercise below will help you make a start.

NOTES ON GRATITUDE

What relationships do I have that others don't?

____

____

____

____

What in life do I take for granted?

____

____

____

____

What freedoms, abilities, or advantages do I have in life that others perhaps don't?

____

____

____

____

What good things in my life does my self-esteem monster want me to forget about?

____

____

____

____

Practicing gratitude is like learning to stretch a muscle. Initially the muscle is tight, often as a result of years of needing to hold tension. Gradual stretching trains the muscle to be more supple so the attached limbs can move with more freedom. Gratitude is similar in that practice is required to develop suppleness, although the benefit of this suppleness is that it allows you to notice the meaning in your life and better appreciate it when you see it.

IN SUMMARY

All of these previous chapters have been building on the idea that you, just as you are, are fundamentally okay; you're not damaged or broken. The pain, the hurt, the memories, and the not-so-great ways you've tried to cope with these—they are not YOU in that they're not woven into the fabric of your DNA. They are your reflections of past and difficult experiences you've been through that you didn't choose. You've done the best you could in difficult circumstances and have survived, for which you deserve credit. Granted, some of your coping strategies have had unintended consequences. But all of this is entirely human, which is to say, nothing here should automatically exclude you from the human race. In fact, it's your very ticket to being human. The relationship you've built up over the years with your self-esteem monster, while incredibly limiting and painful, entirely makes sense. This relationship has protected you, helped you carry on, allowed you to keep living. Well done for getting this far. It just so happens that you have outgrown this relationship. The costs now outweigh the benefits, and it's time to move on.

So far in part 3, we've covered four of the six steps to self-acceptance: mindfully tuning in to the present moment; noticing and observing yourself and your self-stories; making room for and accepting difficult thoughts and feelings; and, in this chapter, six strategies to help you step back from comparing yourself to others. All of this then sets the stage for the question, what next? What do you want to do with your life now? What kind of person do you want to be?

Bringing It All Together

Which of the six acceptance skills covered in this chapter do you feel most drawn to? Put a check mark next to your favorites.

- ☐ Comparison Spotting
- ☐ Time Traveling
- ☐ Reminding Yourself "I Am Here"
- ☐ Stretching Rubber Bands (Practicing New Behaviors)
- ☐ Thanking Your Monster
- ☐ Gratitude Journaling

Now, look at the ones that feel like your least favorite. Consider why this may be the case. What does your monster have to say about these strategies?

____

____

____

CHAPTER 11

Working Out What Matters

While it is usually pretty straightforward to work out *what* it is that we are doing at any given moment, it can be a lot more difficult to work out *why* we are doing it. For example, have you spent most of the current week doing stuff that really makes your heart sing, or has most of it been spent doing things that are kind of mundane but nevertheless feel like they need to be done? Life is always going to be a balance between doing what we *want* to do and doing what we feel we *should* do. However, we are going to suggest that life can be a more enriching experience if you spend more of it tuned in to what really matters to you and letting that be the determinant of your behavior, rather than simply doing what your self-story says you should do. Thus, the *why* question is going to be central to this chapter—and to the fifth step to self-acceptance. *Why* am I doing this? Is it my values or my monster in the driving seat? The idea of trying to live life in accordance with the things that really matter has been mentioned throughout this book. We've bandied this word "values" around a lot. Here's where we will try to unpack the idea of value-driven living with the aim of helping you work out how you truly want to live.

THE COMFORTABLE COMFORT ZONE

The concept of a "comfort zone" is a familiar one. Inside it is a safe place to be, and the idea of staying tucked in there can be a very attractive one. Usually, when we stick with what's comfortable and familiar, our monsters stay relatively quiet, our emotions don't get the better of us, and we can feel reasonably content in the knowledge that we are not taking too many risks. It's a *comfort* zone, right? That's exactly how you might expect it to feel. And... There's always an "and." If we could insert a sad face emoji here, we would, because in this case, the "and" is the understanding that if we spend our entire lives inside the comfort zone, we will miss out on a lot of the things that make life exciting and rewarding. As comfortable as it is in there, there's always that sense that all of those unicorns and rainbows one hears about might just be on the outside, and that we will need to step outside of what's comfortable in order to find them.

The other sad part is the knowledge that for lots of us, our comfort zone is actually more like a prison that our self-stories have trapped us in. The story tells us that we cannot leave and that doing so would bring more fear and discomfort than we could manage. That's the other thing about comfort zones: as much as they are comfortable inside, stepping outside of them immediately gives rise to discomfort. That being the case, we can easily be persuaded by our self-stories to stay inside. The activity below will help you explore whether this idea resonates with you. It might be a tough exercise, so see if you can do it with an extra helping of kindness and warmth (and notice your monster freak out at the prospect of you being kind to yourself).

THE COSTS OF COMFORT

If you recognize that your self-story has persuaded you to stay with what's comfortable and avoid taking on risks or challenges, think about what you have missed out on as a consequence. Perhaps the best way to think about this is to answer the following question:

If my monster had not been holding me back, what might I have done differently?

Use the space below to make some notes about risks you might have taken, challenges you might have accepted, or activities you might have engaged in.

What do you notice when you look at what you have written? What thoughts and feelings are showing up regarding the way your life could have been different? Take a mindful pause and check your responses to the exercise before you carry on reading.

THE PROS AND CONS OF PLAYING IT SAFE

As with everything in life, there is no one simple prescription for striking the balance between time spent in and out of your comfort zone. Clearly, there are advantages and disadvantages to both. We don't know you, the content of your self-story, or your current life circumstances, so it would most likely be very unhelpful for us to prescribe anything. Rather, we would like to invite you to consider what kind of in/out balance you would like to strike for yourself. If you completed the above exercise and concluded that staying inside your comfort zone has served you very well without any obvious costs, then we would probably urge you to carry on with your current strategy, provided you would not perceive any costs of doing so over the longer term. If, on the other hand, you started to notice some sadness or a sense of having missed out, the rest of this chapter might help you to think about what might be worth stepping out of your comfort zone for. After all, if you are going to volunteer to experience discomfort, you'll need a really good reason.

CHOOSING A LIFE WORTH LIVING

Back in chapter 4, we introduced you to the matrix and the idea of toward and away moves. Away moves can often feel like the safer option, with toward moves frequently feeling scary as we step outside of what is comfortable. So, how do we work out what is a good enough reason to get out of our comfort zone? It can be a tricky question to answer at the best of times. It can be much more challenging when buried under the weight of a negative self-story that constantly offers up a narrative that says you're not capable or deserving of a more rewarding life. This is where the concept of values can be useful as a means of discovering, or rediscovering, what it is that makes you tick. There are many ways to discover what our true values might be, and we will run through several below, although as a starting point, consider your responses to the previous exercise. What did you write about what your life could be if your self-story wasn't holding you back? What does that tell you about what matters to you? If you had a totally free hand, what would you choose to prioritize, and why? The answer to these questions starts the journey into understanding what your values really look like.

When we talk about values, we are usually talking about a quality that can be described in a single word, without getting too mind-y about it. Thus, when considering the question of what values are important to us, we can answer without overthinking, and in a manner that minimizes the chances of our self-story getting in the way too much. Values are also qualities that don't really need justification from that thinking part of our mind, and we can simply hold them to be important without having to give reasons. Here are some examples of the kind of things we mean. Take a moment to notice your reactions as you read the list below (also available at http://www.newharbinger.com/43041). Use your tuning in and noticing skills to tune in to the present moment and check in with your reactions and emotions, since they will probably tell you something about what really matters to you as well as what your monster might be dictating.

Adventure	Determination	Loyalty
Authenticity	Fairness	Openness
Autonomy	Faith	Optimism
Community	Fun	Peace
Compassion	Growth	Respect
Connection	Honesty	Responsibility
Contribution	Justice	Security
Courage	Kindness	Self-Care
Creativity	Learning	Spirituality
Curiosity	Love	Trust

Reading the list might prompt you to think of other important values. If it does, make a note of them below.

Do certain values jump out at you because they hold a more personal meaning? Are there some things you feel you *should* value, because that would be the right thing to do? As always, there is no right or wrong way to respond.

Values help to define what sort of person you want to be, what you want to stand for in life, and what motivates you to make changes or pick challenges for yourself. There are a few additional aspects to the concept of values that are important to consider. First, true values are freely chosen, reflecting our desires rather than demands that might be placed upon us, either from others or from our own histories. For example, society might say we should value spirituality, or our self-story might say we don't deserve respect. In considering your own true values, it is helpful to try and let go of these rules and expectations. Here is a short exercise that might help you move toward this.

IT'S A MIRACLE!

Suppose a miracle had occurred and you woke up in a world where your monster loved you unconditionally, and so did everyone else in the world who mattered to you. Since you would automatically have everyone's approval, even your own, you would be free to choose to value whatever you wanted and put those values into action however you saw fit. In this world you would not be held back by the weight of having to keep your monster happy, please others, or conform to social rules.

Go back over the list above and pick three values that you would choose to prioritize, and for each one, think about one way you could put it into practice. If that's too difficult, you could try and do the exercise in reverse by thinking of an action that you would take and then thinking about what choosing that action says to you about which value is important.

Value	Action
Example: *Connection*	*I would make sure I kept in regular contact with my best friend from school.*

Value	Action

What do you notice when you look at what you have written? What thoughts and feelings are showing up regarding the way your life could have been different? Take a mindful pause and check your responses to the exercise before you carry on reading.

While we don't actually live in such a world, maybe it is possible to take some value-driven steps anyway. Remember, the actions don't need to be grand gestures. Small, meaningful steps are just as valuable. The above exercise links to the second important characteristic of values: that they act as a pointer for ongoing patterns of behavior. Put another way, values are something you can enact, rather than just think or feel. Remember that useful compass metaphor from chapter 4? Values are like the points on a compass. They point you in a particular direction, and once you are headed that way, you can choose exactly where to go. Just as there are lots of places to visit if you head west with a compass, if you choose to take your life in the direction of, for example, "connection," there are lots of possible ways to enact this, from meeting friends or texting family members to joining a community group or engaging with an online forum.

Psychological research suggests that increasing the amount of time we spend engaged in value-driven activity (as opposed to just following all of the "shoulds") benefits our overall well-being (e.g., Stockton et al. 2019). You probably know this to be true without having to read any research. You only have to think of the last thing you did because you really wanted to and compare it with the last thing you did only because you had to. We would be willing to bet that the experience of doing those two things was quite different.

Most of us live in cultures that are dominated by the pursuit of goals. Of course, there is nothing intrinsically wrong with having goals in life, it's just that sometimes the pursuit of the goal can take on a life of its own and we forget the reason why the goal was important to us in the first place. We can easily get seduced by chasing the acquisition of things we are supposed to want, such as money or possessions, rather than seeking experiences that really bring meaning to our lives. Also, lots of goals seem to be set for us by some mysterious external force. Have you ever had those questions from people that seem to be prompting you to pursue goals somehow determined by cultural norms? "Are you dating anyone?" is a good example. It seems to be just one in a whole sequence of similar questions that follow from each other, such as "When are you guys going to get married?" "Are you planning to have children?" and "When do you think you'll have another baby?" If we're not careful, we end up chasing goals that aren't even ours and we lose that sense of being present. That's one of the drawbacks of being too goal-focused. Since goals only really exist in the past (ones that we have achieved) or in the future (ones that we are working toward), they don't always help us attend to what's going on in the present. Values, on the other hand, are always in the now and are not something you need to wait around for. Of course, once you work out what matters to you, there is nothing wrong with setting goals to help keep you moving in your valued direction; just stay flexible in thinking about how you might pursue any given value.

CLARIFYING YOUR VALUES

It's all very well for us to give you a definition of values and offer you a list to choose from, as if you could suddenly tune right in to what it is that gives you a reason for living. Experience suggests that things are not this straightforward for many people, and particularly not if you have been burdened by a pervasively negative self-story for any length of time. Returning to our earlier metaphor, this can often be a case of the monster blocking the door. When the struggle against the monster (or allowing yourself to be dictated to by it) has been going on for a while, it is likely that *the monster itself*, rather than anything that might be behind the door, will have been the focus of your attention. If so, the idea of trying to clarify your values might seem somewhat abstract or difficult to get your head around. In this section, we will present a few exercises to help you tune in to what matters, in the service of living life with greater meaning and purpose.

Some of the simplest methods for values clarification involve the use of lists of values or questionnaires. Examples of both are freely available on the internet with a simple search. If you want a list, you could use the one from earlier in this chapter as the basis for the following exercise. Once you have identified which values are important to you, you could start sorting them according to their importance to you (e.g., not very important—somewhat important—very important).

LOVE, WORK, HEALTH, AND PLAY

There are many areas in life where we could helpfully work out where our priorities lie. It can be hard to know where to start, so for now, choose one of the four domains we introduced in chapter 4 (pertaining to quadrant 1 of the matrix) to attend to in order to make some changes:

- Love—the important close relationships in your life (partner/family/friends)
- Work—your current occupational or educational activities
- Health—your physical or psychological well-being
- Play—the part of your life where you pursue recreation or fun activities

One way of thinking about values is that they are a quality of an action. That is, the value suggests a way of doing any given action, for example, being *creative* at work. Read through your chosen values list and pick one value that you would like to bring to the area of life you have selected above. Using the space below, note the area, the value, and one specific action that would be consistent with that value.

Area of Life	**Value**	**Action**
Example: Work	Creativity	To make the layout of the shop window display more colorful

Now, make a few notes about why your chosen value is important and how bringing that quality to your chosen area of life would make a difference to you. Are there people you're aware of who model this value? What do you notice when you think about them?

____

____

____

Finally, take another mindful pause and notice how your thoughts and feelings are responding to the exercise.

Although picking values from a list or a questionnaire can be an easier place to start the process of values clarification, you might find that the values in the list don't resonate with you, perhaps because they don't really reflect your own motivations. The next exercise is a little more challenging, although it has the advantage of prompting you to generate a value yourself rather than pick from a list of predetermined ones.

YOUR TOP TEN MOMENTS

Take a few minutes to write down ten moments from your life that represent you really experiencing life in a way that mattered. They could be big events, such as notable personal achievements or times when you overcame adversity, although they could also be smaller, precious moments. They might be bittersweet memories, in which you experienced poignant or even really difficult emotions but that nevertheless feel important to you in terms of what matters. There are no "correct" responses to this—it will be different for every person. The important thing is for it to be personal for you. Go with your gut and try not to overthink the list. If you can't think of ten, just write down as many as you can.

1. ______________________________
2. ______________________________
3. ______________________________
4. ______________________________
5. ______________________________
6. ______________________________
7. ______________________________
8. ______________________________
9. ______________________________
10. ______________________________

Okay, so that was the easy part. Now we invite you to start trimming your list down. Imagine that something happened and you were no longer able to access the memory of half the items on the list. Put a check mark next to the ones you would choose to keep. Take a pause and notice what thoughts and feelings show up. Does your choice of what to keep start to tell you anything about your priorities? Is your monster piping up too? Notice any self-critical thoughts if they are present. Remember the link between values and pain that we discussed in chapter 9? It is possible that any discomfort you are noticing might also say something about what matters.

Now, imagine something else happened, and this time, two more moments were lost to you, bringing your list down to three things. Choose again, placing a check mark next to the top three moments you would want to keep. Pause again to notice your reactions. Finally, imagine you had to lose another two and could only retain one moment. Which one would it be? Put a check mark next it. What does choosing that one moment tell you about your priorities in life? See if you can put that into just one word and complete the sentence below.

Choosing that one particular moment tells me that one of the values I care most deeply about is

____.

Consider the past few weeks and months. How many times have you taken actions that have been in the service of this value? If you could make any changes over the next few weeks such that your actions were more consistent with the value you have just identified, what would they be?

Finally, take a last mindful pause and notice your thoughts and feelings. What does it feel like to consider your history in this way? What does your monster have to say about it? What does any of that tell you about where your true priorities in life lie?

YOUR VALUES AND YOUR SELF

Hopefully, the previous exercise will have struck a chord with you somewhere along the line and given you some insight into *why* some memories really stand out. Clarifying and connecting with our values is what makes life meaningful. Unfortunately, negative self-stories can often get in the way of that connection, and we can get lost in a fog of fusion and avoidance where we prioritize *not feeling bad* over living a life with meaning and purpose. Simply trying to avoid our pain tends to have an inflexible and constraining quality, whereas moving toward our values frequently feels more flexible and opens up our choices.

One of the main ways in which difficult self-stories can constrain us is in the way we act toward ourselves. While it can often be hard to treat others with kindness and compassion, it is frequently *much* more difficult to relate to ourselves in the same way. We are regularly much meaner to ourselves than to others. For this reason, we want to devote some space to the consideration of the values of compassion and acceptance as applied to ourselves.

When trying to focus on values and act accordingly, our minds are prone to resist, raising objections like *You don't deserve it* and *That's okay for other people, just not for you.* We can get so used to obeying this narrative that our sense of what we truly value becomes remote or gets lost altogether. It might be really hard to sit with this question...and here it comes anyway... When did it become okay to treat *yourself* like that? When did the normal rules of treating human beings in a fair and decent way stop applying to you? A core idea within the concept of self-acceptance is that all human beings have the same intrinsic self-worth. Since we subscribe to this concept, as detailed in chapter 3, we would like to invite you to consider the notion that you are just as worthy of a value-driven life as anyone else on the planet. You have a right to your own personal set of values, whatever they are, and if your self-story objects to that suggestion, maybe now is the time to flex those compassion muscles once again.

We have talked about the benefits of flexible perspective taking in this book already. For example, in chapter 6, in the service of developing self-compassion, we asked you to consider how you would respond to a friend if they were struggling with the issues you face. While it is usually easier to tap into values of compassion and acceptance for a friend, it is also common for our self-stories to get in the way of listening to this same compassionate voice. As suggested above, the monster within us will frequently say that the same rules just don't apply to us and that we are not entitled to the same care and compassion. The following exercise offers a different take on perspective taking in an effort to get around this issue.

THE YOUNGER YOU

That difficult self-story of yours most likely didn't show up for the first time yesterday. It's probably been around for a long time. It's old, maybe even as old as you can remember. See if you can imagine the earliest point in your life when the story said harsh and critical things to you. When did it first get in the way of the things that matter to you? How old were you when it first said that you didn't deserve things to be the way you would like them?

Cast your eyes around wherever you are and look for an empty chair. See if you can picture that much younger version of yourself sitting in the chair. Take some time to build up the image. How old are you? What do you look like? What clothes do you have on? How are you wearing your hair? What if that little one came over to you for help and said out loud the kind of thing that your self-story habitually says: "I'm not good enough," "I don't deserve it," or something similar. Imagine you heard that and saw how unhappy the younger you felt. What would it be like hearing that? What would you feel toward the younger you? Imagine that you could reach through time and give your younger self some kind and wise words, perhaps reflecting some of the skills you have learned in this book. What would you say? Distill into one sentence what you would like to say and write it down below.

____

____

What sentence did you write down? Was it kind? Were you able to find some compassion for your younger self? If you were, perhaps you could practice saying it to yourself when you notice your monster getting in the way of you pursuing your values. Give yourself the same kindness you would extend to a child who was suffering. Living a life guided by values can be very rewarding…and it is not always easy. As we get into the next chapter on putting values and the other skills we have described into action, make sure you bring some self-acceptance and compassion with you on the journey.

IN SUMMARY

We tend to do most of what we do because our thoughts tell us to. The constant swirl of words and thoughts in our heads provides us with reasons and justifications for our decisions, and rarely, if ever, do we stop to ask *why* we do what we do. If all our decisions led us toward a life full of meaning and purpose, this would not be a problem. However, the rules and self-stories we develop over time can make it more difficult to truly live lives of our own making, and if we are not careful, we can become puppets to our monster within.

The process of getting in touch with our values is about trying to find a different determinant of our behavior. Connecting with what really matters can revitalize our choices, and it can mean that life is more about leading with the heart rather than the head. This is not necessarily an easy road, and doing the things we care about for the reasons that matter can mean that our self-stories kick up even more of a fuss. The next chapter will explore the last step to self-acceptance: how to take value-driven actions and manage the internal barriers that inevitably show up.

Bringing It All Together

Pause to think about what this chapter has added to your understanding of values. Has it helped you think about how to choose your actions? Below, note any changes you could make to help you take your life in a more value-driven direction.

____

____

____

CHAPTER 12

Making Bold Moves

So here we are at the start of the final chapter. It seems hard to believe that we're here already. If you're here as well, then we would like to say thank you for sticking with us. We've talked a lot, and while psychologists like us tend to be fond of talking a lot, none of it will be that helpful unless you decide to put your feet down differently in life. The business of behavior change comes down to first deciding that change would be helpful, next picking a direction for that change, and then taking action in that direction. Ultimately, this whole book is only really able to plant some seeds about how you might relate more healthily to yourself and be less encumbered by your self-story. The job of watering those seeds falls to you. Thus, this chapter will cover ways of taking what you have learned from previous chapters and translating it into values-based action—the final step to self-acceptance. We will also remind you of helpful ways of responding if and when your monster objects to the bold new decisions you are making.

CHOOSING TO BUILD THE LIFE YOU WANT

We should be clear from the beginning of this chapter that we are not starting from the assumption that you *need* to change anything. Remember our stance from earlier in the book—you are not broken, and you do not need to be fixed. That said, if any of what you have read has gotten you thinking about areas of your life in which you could choose to operate differently, expand your range of behaviors, or simply make wiser decisions, then perhaps this chapter will give you a bit of a structure for doing just that. Only you will know where you want to start. If you're stuck for inspiration, skip back over the exercises in chapter 4 on using the matrix, chapter 5 on the various self-care domains, or chapter 11 on working out what matters. Wherever you want to make changes, we would gently encourage you to have one eye on the importance of self-care. As the old proverb says, one cannot serve from an empty vessel, so whatever path you want to pursue, try to take a quality of compassion and self-acceptance along for the ride. This is a big ask, and if you are able, we'd invite you to extend that compassion to your monster, since we predict it will kick up more and more of a fuss the farther out of your comfort zone you choose to go. Work through the exercise below to get orientated to the value you want to start with and how to consider self-care along the way.

WRITING ABOUT YOUR VALUES

Take a piece of paper and write either "Love," "Work," "Health," or "Play" at the top of it. Next write a value (e.g., connection, authenticity) that you would like to apply to that area of your life in the service of making a change. Take ten minutes to write about why it is important to you to make a value-driven change in that part of your life. Try not to overthink it—just let it flow as if you were explaining it to someone else. Here are a few questions you can use as prompts as you write:

Why does this value matter to me?

When has it been important in my life?

How would life be more meaningful if I made this value-driven change?

How have I seen it benefit others when they have made the kind of change I am considering?

What might be the cost of not changing?

How can I look after myself in the process?

What are the self-care behaviors I know to be good for me when I'm making changes?

How might I deal with any uncomfortable thoughts and feelings that show up as I try to make this change?

FROM VALUES TO GOALS AND ACTIONS

Pursuing bold moves in the direction of meaningful change involves making two different commitments. The first is the commitment to turn values into action. After all, there's little point in having a value around caring for the environment if you don't ever recycle the plastic that you use. It goes without saying that regular recycling habits serve that value more fully than just remembering on the odd occasion. Therefore, a combination of purpose and persistence emerges as being important in really making a difference.

It is a basic fact of life that learning occurs more quickly when the consequences of our behavior are rewarding. For example, when an infant begins to talk and receives praise and attention from all the adults, that infant will quickly learn that making those sounds leads to good things happening. A child growing up in an environment without that same kind of feedback will take much longer to learn to communicate. Values provide a way of tuning in to these same kinds of immediate rewards, only the rewards are internal (e.g., a sense of fulfilment or of having done the right thing) as opposed to external (e.g., praise).

When we choose to take action based on our values, we tend to be more creative and flexible in how we take that action.

The second commitment is to work to manage the barriers that can so easily obstruct our good intentions. These barriers fall into one of two groups (although one often sneakily masquerades as the other). The first kind are external barriers, where the context in which you find yourself doesn't support you pursuing the kind of action you want to take. Let's say that you have a value of helping people and you decide you want to volunteer to support a reading program in a local school. However, when you approach the school, they tell you that they have enough volunteers already, and anyway, they would not be able to take you because you don't have the appropriate clearance to work with kids. That is a genuine external barrier to your goal of working in the reading program. These kinds of barriers can be worked around as long as you keep your focus on your value. Using the above example, there are lots of different ways of helping people, and if one route is blocked, there will always be others.

Of course, some external barriers, like not having enough time or balancing various responsibilities, can be difficult to navigate, although be mindful to check whether the second kind of barrier isn't just cunningly pretending to be the first. Internal barriers (like thoughts and emotions or difficult self-stories) often present themselves as external barriers. Let's suppose you had been inspired by chapter 5, and in the service of self-care, you had decided to commit to moving your body a bit more by going to the gym. You had bought some gym gear and now you are trying it on. No sooner do you take a look in the mirror that your monster says, "Are you joking? Are you really going out in that? Look at the size of you! What are all the other people in the gym going to think? Do you not realize how super fit they will all be? Well, at least you'll give them some entertainment!" So, you decide you can't go to the gym because your gym gear isn't right, and people will judge you. What is happening here is that your mind is telling you that there are some real external barriers to your making that toward move, although in reality, this is an *internal* barrier. It's your self-story trying to stop you. It is useful to notice these kinds of barriers because, more often than not, these are the ones that will really slow your progress. Thus, part of this commitment might be to use the mindfulness and acceptance techniques from this book as a way of dealing with your self-story when it tries to limit you expanding your life. It might be helpful to go back though the exercises you completed in earlier chapters to find those that you found most helpful before completing the exercise below.

SIX STEPS TO CHANGE

Here is a simple template for structuring your approach to any actions you want to take. It is an extension of the "Love, Work, Health, and Play" exercise in the previous chapter. Just follow the five steps outlined below.

1. Choose an area of life in which you want to take action: love, work, health, or play.
2. Identify a value that you would like to bring to that part of your life. Try to express it in no more than one or two words.
3. Decide on one goal that would enable you to enact that value. Make it something that is specific so that you can clearly say whether you have done it or not (e.g., "to improve my confidence" is not specific enough, whereas "to speak to my boss about my marketing idea" is).
4. Outline the specific actions you will need to take to achieve the goal (e.g., look at my calendar, email my boss about scheduling a meeting, monitor my emails to check for a response).
5. Check in with yourself about the barriers that might get in the way of achieving your goal. Think especially carefully about the internal barriers that your monster is likely to come up with.
6. Make a plan for acting on your value-driven goal, making sure to include any steps you might need to take to manage any barriers.

Now you're good to go. Commit to doing what you have planned and, however it goes, be sure to review it afterward in order to identify what you learned by doing it.

Area of Life	Value	Action

Finally, take another mindful pause and notice how your thoughts and feelings are responding to the exercise.

If you follow the template above and start taking some steps in the direction of your values, you will likely find yourself balancing your attention between the two commitments outlined above, namely the commitment to values-driven action and the commitment to using techniques described in this book to help you manage when internal barriers show up. This is much like riding a bicycle, where constant small movements to the left and right are required in order to maintain your balance and your forward momentum.

The best way to start is by working any new patterns of value-driven behavior into your existing routines. You don't need to completely reinvent the wheel and make huge changes. Rather, you can begin by taking something you already do and doing it differently. To use some basic examples, you might commit to taking the stairs up to the office rather than the elevator or engaging with the sales assistant in the local store instead of hurriedly packing your bag without making eye contact.

NEXT LEVEL MOVES—LEAVING THE COMFORT ZONE BEHIND

If embedding new behaviors into familiar routines goes well, you might want to broaden how you try out new ways of being. The next step is taking on some bigger challenges, perhaps by reclaiming some long-lost areas of your life or even boldly going where you've never gone before. Planned exposure to feared or previously avoided situations is one of the most widely used and best evidenced tools that psychology has. The evidence for its efficacy is excellent, and it is consistent with the theme of this book in that it is all about encouraging you to make "toward" moves while not allowing your monster to hold you back.

One of our favorite researchers, Michelle Craske, has described how people can update their old rules when they engage in new or previously avoided activities (Craske et al. 2014). Essentially, you can revise the rules laid down by your self-story if you are willing to get out of your comfort zone, thereby opening up the possibility of a more fulfilling life. While this is likely to be an effortful and even painful process (much like the effort and pain of exercise after a few months on the couch), it can potentially result in your getting to do more of the things in life that really matter to you. Remember, we are not trying to avoid distress, but rather helping you maximize the ways in which you can learn to embed value-driven behavior in your life. Inspired by the work of Michelle Craske along with a friend and colleague of ours, Eric Morris (2017), below is our research-supported list of how you can take your toward moves to the next level and maximize your learning.

- Ensure that planned activities are connected to your values (e.g., going to a party because you care about showing support for the host rather than going because you think you should).

- Be willing to experience any discomfort that shows up, noticing and observing it, without working to reduce it. Remember the values–pain link: your discomfort is showing up because you're doing something that matters.
- Use your mindfulness skills to stay present during exercises, for example by *describing* and *labeling* uncomfortable internal experiences as they happen, rather than avoiding them (e.g., *I notice feeling anxious…oh…and there's my monster saying what a loser I am for being so scared).*
- Be curious about what you are learning during new activities while letting go of the idea that there is anything you have to get right.
- Practice doing new things without any old "away" behaviors (e.g., rituals) that you usually use to keep yourself feeling safe. These behaviors tend to interfere with learning about what you are really capable of because if you do happen to succeed, you will be likely to attribute that success to the ritual rather than your own efforts.
- Vary your activities in terms of the challenges they present (e.g., something difficult one week and something easier the next). Our learning is boosted when the mismatch between what we expect and what we actually experience is at its greatest.
- Try doing the same thing in lots of different contexts so that what you learn about yourself and your capabilities is not confined to one particular type of situation (e.g., if you're going to experiment with being more assertive, try it at home, at work, and in your relationships with your friends).

POTENTIAL BANANA SKINS

Taking action can be difficult, and there are a number of things that can lead us to slip up. In this section, we will run through a few of the common ones.

The Monster Objects

If you find that your monster starts giving you a hard time as you move toward a values-driven goal, this is 100% to be expected. It would be strange if it didn't happen. Remember, in your pain you find your values, and in your values you find your pain. It is also helpful to remember that values are something that you freely choose and that working toward them is also a choice, rather than something that your self-story says you *must* do. It might sound like an odd thing to say, but our values provide us with a good reason to suffer. To return to the idea of the monster that blocks the door, values describe what is "behind the door," and if you start walking through, you can expect the monster to object. Perhaps try to hold on to the idea that it's only trying to protect you from danger and doesn't mean to cause you harm. Seeing it this way might help you respond compassionately to any objections it might raise to your bold moves forward.

Psychologist Steven C. Hayes (2019) offered a radical approach to dealing with your mind's resistance to making change: developing "reverse compass" habits. The idea is to carefully listen to your self-story objecting. Where does it say you cannot go? What does it say is beyond your capability? What does it say that you absolutely must not do? Because of the relationship between your values and your discomfort, the answers to these questions might tell you something about what really matters. Once you have worked out what the resistance is telling you about what matters, the task is to do the *reverse* of what your mind says you should do. For example, if your monster is saying you absolutely must not trust your best friend with that thing you've been worrying about, maybe that tells you that trust is really important in your friendship. Would you want your best friend to feel like they could trust you if they had the same worry? Then maybe you could let your monster say what it wants to say, thank it for trying to help, and then go and have that talk with your friend.

Taking Things Too Far Too Soon

First, we can end up being so courageous that we step too far outside of what is comfortable too quickly. This can end up scaring the life out of us so that all we want to do is get right back inside that comfort zone and never come out again. If you were going to train to run a marathon, you probably wouldn't run twenty-six miles on your first training session—you would start with something consistent with the twenty-six-mile goal while making sure it was achievable given your current level of fitness. Similarly, our advice would be to start small. You could ask yourself, *What is the smallest meaningful step I could take toward my values today?* and commit to doing that first. Imagine a comfort zone, and see if you can picture a self-care zone surrounding it, like two concentric circles. Pick goals that are outside the comfort zone but inside the self-care zone. It really doesn't matter how small the step you choose to take is—all of it counts as progress.

The second problem is getting caught up with the idea that you must pursue your values all the time, such that you end up taking value-driven actions at times when you are not up to it or when conditions don't support it. This is like the person who turns up for work when they have a virus because they are rigidly adhering to their value of working hard. Turning the flexible notion of freely chosen values into a rigid rule like this can be counterproductive; that person runs the risk of becoming even more ill as well as passing on the virus to their co-workers. Choosing to relax our grip on our values, holding them lightly, and being flexible in how we choose toward and away moves is generally better for our well-being.

Something Goes Wrong

Taking value-driven action is not about never slipping or never lapsing back into unhelpful habits. You *will* slip up and you *will* fall back under the monster's spell from time to time. You might find that your monster loves these moments, using them as a great opportunity to remind you about what a loser you are and laughing at you for ever thinking you could make a different life for yourself. This is all completely normal. Two steps forward, one step back, as the old saying goes. Another saying, sometimes used within the military, suggests "It's not about how you fall, it's about how you get up." We would encourage you to think less about what went wrong and more about how you are going to choose to respond to it.

While we can never change what just happened, we can take responsibility for what is about to happen, and the next move is always a choice. There is an elegant account of an interaction between the psychologist Kelly Wilson and someone whom he was trying to help with managing his substance use (Hayes 2019) that speaks to this issue. Contrary to his goals, the client had used opiates again, and his self-story was telling him what a failure he was. Kelly simply asked him, "Which of your values have changed?" to which the client reflected that none of them had—he still valued sobriety and wanted a life without using substances. Kelly then outlined two clear choices in terms of the patterns of behavior the client could work on strengthening and asked him which he wanted to adopt: "Commit—slip—quit" or "Commit—slip—commit." If you find yourself slipping up, maybe you could ask yourself the same question.

IN SUMMARY

So, that's the end of our six steps to self-acceptance. This chapter has focused on using everything we have covered and putting it into action. It is key to remember that we move with our feet, and all the good intentions in the world matter little unless we are prepared to put our feet down differently as we move through life. Making the choice to do things differently is important, although not as important as actually doing it. We have outlined the significance of using values as the compass for action. We have also described how other mindfulness and acceptance skills are important in making bold moves, since doing so almost always involves stepping outside of the constraints that your self-story has placed upon you over the years. As you continue to practice your bold moves, you start to change your relationship with your self-esteem monster. Where previously the monster had important work to do every time you thought about taking a bold move, now you don't need it to keep yourself safe. The monster has run out of top tips for you and is out of work and moving into retirement.

We should restate that there is no imperative to change anything unless you believe doing so would be helpful. If change is the choice that you make, we hope that you move forward showing the same kindness and compassion to yourself that you would show to someone you love dearly.

Bringing It All Together

What have you taken from this chapter? How has it helped you bring together any learning from previous chapters? Most importantly, what will you do once you finally put this book down? Taking all you have read here into account, if you could make a commitment to yourself now, what would it be? Use the space below to write your responses to these or other questions that you notice showing up. And then, using the skills you have learned, if you so choose, put your feet down differently and make some bold moves toward living a life of your choosing.

____

____

____

____

____

Acknowledgments

This book is based on the principles of acceptance and commitment therapy (ACT—pronounced as one word; Hayes, Strosahl, and Wilson 1999). ACT is a scientific model of human behavior that focuses on all things that humans do—from our greatest achievements to the places we get most stuck in life. By scientific, we mean that there is a large amount of research evidence that sits underneath the model. At the time of writing, there are over 300 randomized controlled trials attesting to the effectiveness of the model.

A wide community of researchers, practitioners and clinicians influenced our ideas and thinking in the development of this book. These people largely come together as part of the Association for Contextual Behavioral Science (ACBS), which is the "mothership" for all ACT-related things. We are hugely indebted to everyone in and around the ACT community for their support and inspiration.

We also want to thank our editors at New Harbinger, Tesilya Hanauer, Vicraj Gill, and Rona Bernstein, for all their fantastic input in helping us craft the manuscript into shape.

Most importantly, we would like to acknowledge the wisdom and courage of everyone who has ever sat across from either one of us in a therapy room. Without your willingness to be vulnerable and trust us with your stories, we would never have learned most of what fills the pages of this book.

References

Bartholomew, R. 2001. *Little Green Men, Meowing Nuns and Head-Hunting Panics: A Study of Mass Psychogenic Illness and Social Delusion.* Jefferson, NC: Macfarland & Company.

Beck, P. 2016. *The War of the Worlds: From H. G. Wells to Orson Welles, Jeff Wayne, Steven Spielberg and Beyond.* London: Bloomsbury Academic.

Baumeister, R. F., J. D. Campbell, J. I. Krueger, and K. D. Vohs. 2003. "Does High Self-Esteem Cause Better Performance, Interpersonal Success, Happiness, or Healthier Lifestyles?" *Psychological Science in the Public Interest* 4, no. 1 (May): 1–44.

Branden, N. 1969. *The Psychology of Self-Esteem.* Los Angeles: Nash Publishing.

Brown, B. (2012). *Daring Greatly: How the Courage to Be Vulnerable Transforms the Way We Live, Love, Parent, and Lead.* New York: Gotham Books.

Ciarrochi, J., A. Bailey, and R. Harris. 2015. *The Weight Escape.* London: Constable and Robinson Ltd.

Craske, M. G., M. Treanor, C. Conway, T. Zbozinek, and B. Vervliet. 2014. "Maximizing Exposure Therapy: An Inhibitory Learning Approach." *Behaviour Research and Therapy* 58 (July): 10–23.

Ellis, A. 2005. The Myth of Self-Esteem: *How Rational Emotive Behavior Therapy Can Change Your Life Forever.* New York: Prometheus

Flynn, J. 2005. *War of the Worlds: From Wells to Spielberg.* New York: Galactic Books.

Gilbert, P., ed. 2005. *Compassion: Conceptualisations, Research and Use in Psychotherapy.* New York: Routledge.

Harari, Y. N. 2014. *Sapiens: A Brief History of Humankind.* London: Harvill Secker.

Harris, R. 2009. *ACT Made Simple: An Easy-To-Read Primer on Acceptance and Commitment Therapy.* Oakland, CA: New Harbinger.

Hayes, S. C. 2019. *A Liberated Mind: How to Pivot Toward What Matters.* New York: Avery.

Hayes, S. C., K. D. Strosahl, and K. G. Wilson. 1999. *Acceptance and Commitment Therapy: An Experiential Approach to Behavior Change.* New York: Guilford Press.

Keng, S. L., M. J. Smoski, and C. J. Robins. 2011. "Effects of Mindfulness on Psychological Health: A Review of Empirical Studies." *Clinical Psychology Review* 31, no. 6 (August): 1041–1056.

Khoury, B., T. Lecomte, G. Fortin, M. Masse, P. Therien, Bouchard, V., M. A. Chapleau, K. Paquin, and S. G. Hofmann. 2013. "Mindfulness-Based Therapy: A Comprehensive Meta-Analysis." *Clinical Psychology Review* 33, no. 6 (August): 763–771.

Kimmes, J. G., J. A. Durtschi, and F. D. Fincham. 2017. "Perception in Romantic Relationships: A Latent Profile Analysis of Trait Mindfulness in Relation to Attachment and Attributions." *Mindfulness* 8, no. 5: 1328–1338.

McHugh, L., I. Stewart, and P. Almada. 2019. *A Contextual Behavioral Guide to the Self.* Oakland, CA: New Harbinger.

Meadows, G. 2014. *The Sleep Book.* London: Orion.

Morris, E. 2017. *So Long to SUDs – Exposure Is Not About Fear Reduction…It's About New Learning and Flexibility.* http://drericmorris.com/2017/01/13/nosuds/

National Health Service. 2016. *Five Steps to Mental Wellbeing.* https://www.nhs.uk/conditions/stress-anxiety-depression/improve-mental-wellbeing/

National Health Service. 2018. *Benefits of Exercise.* https://www.nhs.uk/live-well/exercise/exercise-health-benefits

Polk, K. L., B. Schoendorff, M. Webster, and F. O. Olaz. 2016. *The Essential Guide to the ACT Matrix: A Step-By-Step Approach to Using the ACT Matrix Model in Clinical Practice.* Oakland, CA: New Harbinger.

"Ruby Wax Talks About a Sane New World." May 1, 2015. *Birmingham What's On.* https://www.whatsonlive.co.uk/birmingham/interviews/ruby-wax-talks-about-a-sane-new-world/2125

Sapolsky, R. 2004. *Why Zebras Don't Get Ulcers,* 3rd ed. New York: Holt.

Sartre, Jean-Paul. (1944) 1989. *No Exit and Three Other Plays.* New York: Vintage International.

Stockton, D., S. Kellett, R. Berrios, F. Sirois, N. Wilkinson, G. and Miles. 2019. "Identifying the Underlying Mechanisms of Change During Acceptance and Commitment Therapy (ACT): A Systematic Review of Contemporary Mediation Studies." *Behavioral and Cognitive Psychotherapy* 47, no. 3 (May): 332–362.

Swain, J., K. Hancock, C. Hainsworth, and J. Bowman. 2013. "Acceptance and Commitment Therapy in the Treatment of Anxiety: A Systematic Review." *Clinical Psychology Review* 33, no. 8 (December): 965–978.

Wilson, K. 2013. *Evolution Matters: A Practical Guide for the Working Clinician.* Keynote address at the First Acceptance and Commitment Therapy and Contextual Behavioural Science Conference, London, UK.

Wilson, T. D., D. A. Reinhard, E. C. Westgate, D. T. Gilbert, N. Ellerbeck, C. Hahn, C L. Brown, and A. Shaked. 2014. "Just Think: The Challenges of the Disengaged Mind." *Science* 345, no. 6192: 75–77.

Joe Oliver, PhD, is a consultant clinical psychologist and joint director of the cognitive behavioral therapy (CBT) for psychosis postgraduate diploma program at University College London. He also works within a North London National Health Service Trust, developing training and delivering interventions for people with psychosis. He is founder of Contextual Consulting, a London-based consultancy offering acceptance and commitment therapy (ACT)-focused training, supervision, and psychological therapy. Joe is an Association for Contextual Behavioral Science (ACBS) peer-reviewed ACT trainer, and regularly delivers ACT teaching and training in the UK and internationally. He is coeditor of *Acceptance and Commitment Therapy and Mindfulness for Psychosis,* and coauthor of *ACTivate Your Life* and *Acceptance and Commitment Therapy.*

Richard Bennett, ClinPsyD, works as a clinical psychologist and cognitive behavioral psychotherapist. He lectures at the Centre for Applied Psychology at the University of Birmingham, where he leads the postgraduate diploma program in CBT. He worked in adult and forensic mental health services in the National Health Service for over twenty years before setting up Think Psychology, an independent psychology practice offering therapy, supervision, and training. Richard is an active member of ACBS and the British Association of Behavioural and Cognitive Psychotherapies (BABCP). He is recognized as a BABCP-accredited psychotherapist, supervisor, and trainer; and an ACBS peer-reviewed ACT trainer. He coedited *Rational Emotive Behavior Therapy in Sport and Exercise,* and is coauthor of *Acceptance and Commitment Therapy.*

Foreword writer **Russ Harris** is an internationally acclaimed ACT trainer; and author of the ACT-based self-help book, *The Happiness Trap.*

MORE BOOKS from NEW HARBINGER PUBLICATIONS

CHILDREN OF THE SELF-ABSORBED, THIRD EDITION
A Grown-Up's Guide to Getting Over Narcissistic Parents
978-1572245617 / US $17.95

DON'T BELIEVE EVERYTHING YOU FEEL
A CBT Workbook to Identify Your Emotional Schemas & Find Freedom from Anxiety & Depression
978-1684034802 / US $21.95

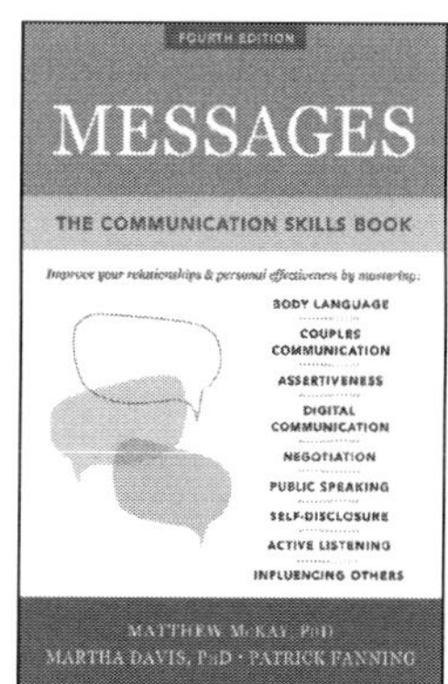

MESSAGES, FOURTH EDITION
The Communication Skills Book
978-1684031719 / US $21.95

THE BODY IMAGE WORKBOOK, SECOND EDITION
An Eight-Step Program for Learning to Like Your Looks
978-1572245464 / US $25.95

THE HIGHLY SENSITIVE PERSON'S GUIDE TO DEALING WITH TOXIC PEOPLE
How to Reclaim Your Power from Narcissists & Other Manipulators
978-1684035304 / US $16.95

THE ACT WORKBOOK FOR DEPRESSION & SHAME
Overcome Thoughts of Defectiveness & Increase Well-Being Using Acceptance & Commitment Therapy
978-1684035540 / US $22.95

 newharbingerpublications

1-800-748-6273 / newharbinger.com

(VISA, MC, AMEX / prices subject to change without notice)

Follow Us

Don't miss out on new books in the subjects that interest you.
Sign up for our **Book Alerts** at **newharbinger.com/bookalerts**

Register your **new harbinger** titles for additional benefits!

When you register your **new harbinger** title—purchased in any format, from any source—you get access to benefits like the following:

- Downloadable accessories like printable worksheets and extra content
- Instructional videos and audio files
- Information about updates, corrections, and new editions

Not every title has accessories, but we're adding new material all the time.

Access free accessories in 3 easy steps:

1. Sign in at NewHarbinger.com (or **register** to create an account).
2. Click on **register a book**. Search for your title and click the **register** button when it appears.
3. Click on the **book cover or title** to go to its details page. Click on **accessories** to view and access files.

That's all there is to it!

If you need help, visit:

NewHarbinger.com/accessories